I Don't Want To Be Alone

For Men And Women Who
Want To Heal
Addictive Relationships

John Lee

Health Communications, Inc.
Deerfield Beach, Florida

John Lee
Austin Men's Center
Austin, Texas

©1990 John Lee
ISBN 1-55874-065-1

Publisher: Health Communications, Inc.
          3201 S.W. 15th Street
          Deerfield Beach, Florida 33442

Cover Design by Reta Thomas

Acknowledgments

I want to thank first of all my clients and workshop participants who taught me so much about myself.

I also want to thank a group of people who have inspired, enlightened and educated me over the last few years. Their lives and work helped make my life work and this book possible:

Pia Mellody for her pioneering work in Co-dependency. Anne Wilson Schaef for her incredible book, *When Society Becomes an Addict*. Charles Whitfield for his support and work, *Healing The Child Within*. John Bradshaw for his ground-breaking insights into family systems and shame. Janet Woititz for her work on Adult Children of Alcoholics. Melody Beattie for her bestseller, *Co-dependent No More*. Wayne Kritsberg for his wisdom, friendship and work, *Adult Children of Alcoholics Syndrome*. Richard Lewis for a very important soon-to-be published work, *The Abandoned Heart*, and a special thanks to all my other many teachers and friends, particularly Dan Jones, Bill Stott, Mary Jackson, Caleb Curren, Scott Lockhart, Allen Maurer, John Hunger, Debi Cope and Maya, Molly Serafin and all the people at the Austin Men's Center.

Dedicated to
Jimmy Lee

Who Makes These Changes?

Who makes these changes?
I shoot an arrow right.
It lands left.
I ride after a deer and find myself
chased by a hog.
I plot to get what I want
and end up in prison.
I dig pits to trap others
and fall in.

I should be suspicious
of what I want.

Rumi
from This Longing
Barks & Moyne

Contents

Preface		ix
1	The Opening	1
2	The Beginning	3
3	The Middle	37
4	The Ending	105
5	New Beginnings	119
6	Postscript	125

Preface

Every child is afraid of being alone, which to them is the fear of death itself. To the child left alone as an infant, each minute had seemed like a lifetime, each hour an eternity.

For every child who was left (look around you, there are millions) there is an adult frozen with fear that it will happen again. This book is for those who were left alone and swore silently to themselves that they would gain all the control they could to keep that feeling from ever entering their body again.

The fear of being alone is basic and primal in the child, but produces chaos and co-dependency in the adult who is ruled by it. There is a way out of this cruelty to ourselves and each other which we now call co-dependency. There is a way to break out of addiction-based relationships once they're recognized as such, whether they are with partners, parents, friends, employers, employees and, yes, even your own children.

This book will provide a large missing piece of the puzzle of recovery from the traumas of childhood and the resulting dependency on people and things to make us feel worthwhile. In this book you'll not only find useful tools and information to help you heal your addictive/co-dependent relationships, you'll also find yourself and the people you love.

Recovery is a process, and each person makes the journey in their own time and way. This book will help you on your journey. It will help you discover the many destructive ways we set up situations and relationships to keep us free from the fear of being alone, only to find ourselves again and again feeling abandoned and abused. This book clearly shows how to stop the cycle of pain and break old patterns that keep us from getting the same old outcome.

I don't want to be alone and I know you don't either. Join me as I share with you my journey — my feelings, insights and victory over the fear of being left alone.

The Opening

"I understand now." That's what I'd say to Laural if she would only listen. I'd tell her that I feel some of what she felt. And I'd tell her everything that has happened and that I have learned since I described our painful love for each other in my first book, *The Flying Boy: Healing the Wounded Man.*

But I can't tell her. The anger, pain and hurt run too deep. After all the pain I went through and detailed in my first book, I still did not understand or feel her pain until the last year and a half of my life. And, thus, two years ago I could only write half of the story. I could not see her side. And while I'm proud of my first book and thankful for the thousands of lives it touched, I must say that if I had it to do all over again and could feel what I feel today, it would be done differently. Laural would not appear so one-dimensional, she so sane and I so sick, she so saintly and I so sinful.

I can't tell her, so I'll tell you. Perhaps you'll put the stories together and see your wounds, your patterns and your pain, and you'll examine them before you hurt yourself or get hurt by another. If you keep reading, you'll see a way out. You'll find some healing by finding yourself and reclaiming your past — and thus your present — and you'll move farther down the path to reclaiming your sometimes lost, wandering soul.

The Beginning

Lucy and I got together and found out that her dreams were my dreams. That night in the Hyde Park Bar and Grill, everything that she or I said was answered by, "Me, too." After two dozen "Me, too's," we started a journey together that moved us toward each other, deeper into ourselves. It is still moving toward a deeper healing for me, as well as a deeper awareness of an illness I have had all my life and didn't even know the name of.

The night dreams and prayers and the "Me, too's" turned into a nightmare. Her original dream of tenderness and coming together with a man, and mine of sharing a life with a woman I saw as an equal in every way were shattered by a disease I had unwittingly been exposed to as a child.

The disease is subtle and did not appear at first. Instead, what appeared were a beautiful woman, letters in my mailbox that were like small literary masterpieces and, later, me standing in a Mississippi airport with a fear as big as Texas.

As I approached her that day from the runway, I could feel and see that something was wrong. There was a tightness in my stomach and tension in my neck. I ignored the physical signals that said this was unsafe and, "You've been here before." Even though I spent several years getting my body back and learning to listen to its messages, knowing it to be the storehouse of memories and information, I chose not to listen. I did so because, even not fully present, this woman was one of the most special people I had ever met and I knew I wanted to be with her. So I refused to listen and convinced myself to stay, though my heart said, "Run, fly or walk very fast, but leave." I stayed. In a way I'm glad I did. I had to learn what I learned.

Lucy gave me a half-hearted hug. I could feel the tightness in her shoulders and could smell her fear. With the fears and the suitcases packed securely into her car, we set off on a weekend journey that seemed like an eternity for two grownups who right before each other's eyes kept turning into six-year-olds.

We passed pleasant conversation, and I wondered where the woman was who had written those open and honest letters and made the phone calls that soothed my soul. This woman with me was a bit chilly, very distant and just not there most of the time. At least this was the way I felt.

The next day we were in a cafeteria trying to eat lunch, picking at overly cooked squash and not eating the stuff that passed for dessert. We looked at our plates instead of each other and then finally went to a nearby park. Before we left the cafeteria, Lucy dropped the first bomb which landed right in my stomach. Staring into space, she said, "I don't know how much longer I'm going to be here in Mississippi."

"What do you mean? I thought you were committed to working here for some time."

"I don't know, I've been thinking a lot lately about New Mexico. There is a wonderful place called the Lama Foundation, and I have been wanting to live and work there for a long time. I think it would do me some good."

It was about this time that my stomach started turning and tightening up in knots. As my stomach cramped, my legs got weak as she talked about leaving. All I could feel was the fear of being left. I had had these feelings before, when Laural left me two and one-half years earlier. I got sick then with stomach cramps and a temperature of 104 degrees, and no doctor in town could diagnose my disease.

Finally, after hearing Lucy say the word "leaving," for what must have been to my fearful ears the millionth time, I excused myself and went into the bathroom. Looking into the mirror, I saw a little boy's face, white with fear underneath a beard gray with age. I then proceeded to throw up.

When I returned to the table, I was only half there, half gone and wholly terrified. I knew this reaction had little to do with the woman I barely knew, who sat through the rest of her meal looking at me, wondering where I had disappeared to.

The rest of the weekend was a disaster. I ducked in and out of bathrooms and in and out of a thousand places in my past. Later that afternoon, I looked deep into her blue-brown eyes and said, "Lucy, I think we ought to just be friends. That's all I can do right now is just be friends."

I knew as I was saying this that it was a lie. True, I wanted her friendship, but the lie I spoke was a way to escape a threatening situation. I knew that if I stayed even in the near proximity of this woman, I would have to face fears and patterns that I had been avoiding all my life. I didn't want just friendship. I felt ready for a mate. While I thought I was not projecting much at this point, I could see that beyond those fears and patterns was not only potential but real possibility. Yet I said, "Let's be friends." And what I meant by that was, "I'm out of here." She looked at me as if she didn't believe me. And, as soon as the words came out, I knew they weren't true. They were just vehicles to sweep me to safety.

The next morning I got up early. The sun was out and there was a touch of coolness in Lucy's demeanor. I took a walk before breakfast. She was in her study, a little sanctuary she had carved out for herself in an old abandoned schoolhouse. Her special place was equipped with a stove and breakfast stuff. We ate in silence. There was a moment at the end of our meal when I slipped silently through the window pane and out into the Southern sky as tears slid down my face. I realized how scared I was, how beautiful she was. I came back into the room. "Lucy, I don't know how to do this. I don't want to be alone. But I don't know how to be with someone."

She looked at me softly from a place of understanding. Those tears were gifts to her and myself that first weekend. We would exchange much more in the months to come, but those were the first.

Lucy took me to the airport, and I thought I'd never see her again. The weekend was so different than the "we" in our letters had planned. I was glad to be leaving a lady I knew was special but I knew I should not be with. I knew I didn't know how to be with her, and I knew she couldn't be with me. So we said our goodbyes. As I flew home, I felt free. For the first time in three days my stomach felt normal. The tension was out of my shoulders. I was sad, but alone and back on familiar ground and in an old pattern. It seemed leaving and being left were all I had ever known.

I learned to leave as a smart dog learns tricks to get what it might not otherwise. I learned to leave when my alcoholic father's temper flared and the yelling started. I'd go into my bedroom, my first retreat, my own private world. The radio would be turned up as loud as possible to tune out the terror in the living room, and I'd turn on the television in hopes it would drown out the sounds of fighting and dull the aches only fear could produce. During my teens the drinking and fighting got worse, and I learned to crawl into a place deep inside me, a place in my mind. There I would black out a world that didn't make sense and try to think away the hurt and pain.

I know, somewhere in all that, I all but lost my ability to be with people and trust them, since if I wasn't leaving, I was being left. Dad was always at work. When he was home, he was either working on the house or in the yard, or he'd be in a place somewhere hidden and lost back behind his eyes from too much alcohol, work, worry or television. Mom was often just as worried, sick, tired or terrified, and little of her energy could be directed to meet my needs.

I all but disappeared, and so did they. I hid in my room, or I'd leave my body in the presence of two adults who in many ways were just children themselves. And I waited for them or me to grow up or for something to change. I waited for Dad to stop drinking, for Mom to take us away from the insanity, or at the very least for Jesus' Second Coming.

Later I waited for some woman to come into my life and love me in ways that Dad and Mom couldn't. Instead, I got women who loved me a lot like Dad and Mom — too little, like Dad, and too much, like Mom. Dad never stopped drinking, Mom stayed with him and Jesus never showed up. But I kept waiting, and in the process I became very passive.

It didn't take me long to realize that although I was responsible for making my life work, I did learn a lot of my passive behavior from my mother. She waited nearly her whole life for the love the storybooks of her childhood had promised — a promise that couldn't be kept. Instead, dollars turned into alcohol and the alcohol was poured into her would-be Prince Charming. Mom took the position that many women took in her generation and some still do. "Stand by your man," "for better or worse," "until death do us part." Mom put her life on hold. She became sick more often than most; migraine headaches seemed to be one of her many exits from the insanity created by alcoholism. But I watched her wait and wither — always praying Dad would stop drinking — always unknowingly playing a part in his alcoholism. I watched her wait and wondered why God had placed this cross on her — never looking at her own family of origin where years before, alcohol had claimed her own father's life. And I watched her wait on Dad hand and foot and wait for him to decide it was time to take a vacation or move or make love. Mom waited. In the meantime, I tried to be all the things Dad couldn't be. My needs waited, and *I* began waiting on her hand and foot when she was sick. *I* became her savior and her caretaker — good practice to be a co-dependent counselor.

I was working with a men's group in Santa Fe one night. Ron was working on his own passivity and tendency to wait on life to come to him. I asked him what he wanted more than anything at that moment. His face flushed and sweat popped out as he said, "To be loved and to be held." He said he always hoped some day his father and mother would be there for him, to hold him and love him. They were both dead now. It didn't look as if he would ever have his wish.

I asked him to say the words, "Please, Mom and Dad, come love and hold me." He sat there for several minutes repeating the phrase. Tears flowed. I asked him if it felt like Mom and Dad were going to come; he said, "No." I then asked him who in the group would he like to have hold him. He immediately pointed to Tom, a gentle-faced man in the corner. I signaled Tom (without Ron's knowledge) not to come no matter what. I asked Ron to begin asking Tom to come hold him. He began doing so and once again the tears began to flow. He finally turned to me and said, "It doesn't look like he's going to come. Maybe I should go over to him and ask him to hold me."

We all breathed a sigh of relief as Ron got up very slowly and cautiously went to a person who might give him what he needed. Tom readily embraced Ron and told him he loved him very much. Ron took himself out of his passivity and out of his pain. At the same time, he helped each man there see how passive we all can be and how we wait and want a wish to come true, instead of walking through our fears to make our needs known and met.

I didn't have to wait long before I received a letter from Lucy telling me how much she appreciated my coming to Mississippi and being willing to risk an encounter with a bona fide adult child of an alcoholic. In her letter she playfully presented fantasy headlines from the local newspaper: "Two Adult Children of Alcoholics Meet & Nearly Die From a Rare Form of Suffocation Due to Overexposure to Self-Analysis." I laughed, still not knowing how close the fantasy was to fact. But the letter was warm and tender. In it she once again opened up to me like a flower, and I found myself looking forward to the next visit she was proposing. I told myself that the last weekend together was a fluke, not a sign of failure, and that this next visit would reaffirm my belief that we were indeed soulmates. Everything would work out fine.

This idea of soulmates has always appealed to me and, I think, to most adult children from dysfunctional families. I'm not saying that soulmates don't exist; it's just that I've had about 20 already and many of my friends and clients have had more. Now I know, according to the books on the subject, you can have more than one. But it seems as if I find one almost immediately after the last one leaves — sometimes before the sheets get changed or her furniture is moved out.

The other day one of my recovering alcoholic friends was saying, "John, I met this woman in San Francisco and I felt like I'd known her my whole life." I winced a little and thought to myself, "Here it comes — soulmate #33." He continued, "I told her, Look, this is not a line, but I feel like I've known you very deeply somewhere before; and she looked into my eyes and said 'I feel the same way.' "

Now, I'm not going to judge, but I am going to present some facts. This man has been divorced three times and had only just the week before broken up with his last girl friend of about six months. Get the picture? No time for grieving the loss of the last relationship. Perhaps no need to — but one week?

This idea of soulmate bothers me a little because it has justified so much and sounds so much like the older idea of looking for one's "other half" or "better half" instead of looking into oneself to find it. For me, soulmate has usually equalled projection. In Jungian terms, *anima* is the feminine aspect or energy in all men. *Animus* is the masculine aspect in all women. Men tend to project this feminine soul onto women and women their masculine soul onto men, instead of accepting this aspect of themselves. Two halves come together, but instead of becoming whole, they usually split in three to six months and go off in search of soulmate #34.

The evenings we spent talking on the phone before Lucy's visit were enchanting and the conversation flowed, because over the phone we built no dams. The minutes turned into hours and I didn't care if AT&T had to repossess my car to pay the bill. We talked openly about love and life and everything in between. I believed this woman was the one, because we were in such agreement about almost everything and we were so much alike.

Finally the day came that she was to arrive. She called and said she couldn't leave Mississippi that day and it would be the next afternoon before she could get there. She said it would be around three or four p.m. Six p.m. came — no Lucy, no call. Seven p.m. — Lucy called and said she had some trouble getting off that day and she was just leaving Mississippi. One-thirty a.m. — she arrived. I was tired and yet fully alert and glad to see her. I had run a tub of hot water for her just moments before she arrived as the warmest welcome I could think of. She came in exhausted, slid into the tub, and we talked and went to bed. But not as lovers. This was one thing that convinced me this time would be different.

Weeks before, when Lucy and I made our second date, she had come prepared for lovemaking. I was not. I had decided before meeting Lucy that my next lover was going to be first my friend and that if we could put the emphasis on friendship, loving sex could easily follow. I had realized that I had always fallen in love with women and/or their bodies before I even knew who they were. I was determined this would not happen again, especially with Lucy. It was made a bit easier by the fact that at first I wasn't that physically attracted to her. One more pattern broken.

I told her all of this, and I could tell that it took her off-guard and touched her deeply. We decided we would first turn our sleeping-together times into an experience more like two kids staying over at each other's houses. And it was great. When we would go to bed, we'd play, we'd wrestle with each other and hold each other. We read one another children's books, poetry and healing prose; one of the nicest things I'd ever done in bed. It was wonderful.

And yet when Lucy finally did get to my house this time, it was so much like the last time I visited her that I just couldn't see it or feel it. I needed to deny it. She wasn't really with me. She was always so open and loving on the phone, but as she prepared to go to bed that night it was as if a soul-snatcher had come and left this woman's body in my bed. She was scared and tired, and she knew it. In her own way, she apologized, but even she didn't fully see how little of her was left to hold a man who was ready to learn to love for the first time.

The mornings were spent talking. I was an early riser and would always want to talk about the past weeks or the present pains. When I'd get up, I'd make waves in the waterbed or breathe a heavy sigh to try to wake her so we could talk. Often she would wake up half heartedly, being the late-night person, late-morning sleeper that she was.

When she would rise I'd find myself most often preparing breakfast, putting on just the right morning music and bringing coffee to her bed. And I loved doing it. It kind of reminded me of my mother.

Most men and women want in part to be taken care of like children, but if you do take care of them, they will hate and perhaps destroy you. A man looks for his mother in many of the women he is attracted to. But that is the boy, the child in the man. The man in him looks for a woman, an equal. If she becomes a mother to him, he will take it for a while and then go off in pursuit of a lover. A man finds it very difficult to make love to a mother because the child within knows that he's not supposed to. And if he doesn't leave because staying is too comfortable or leaving too scary, he stays but disappears behind newspapers, television, work, alcohol, drugs or into old age before his time.

Women very often seek men to pick up where their fathers left off, even though they also want to actualize their full potential. But this is much too difficult to do while one is being taken care of by a parent roughly her own age. While women, too, love being taken care of in some ways, they very often will punish the partner who tries to be the parent. They, too, will seek an equal, resorting to the pursuit of a lover in their dreams, fantasies or the night clubs. Or else they turn into tired old women and, at worst, witches — resembling the Wicked Witch of the North who hates youth and makes unreal demands.

I remember my mother taking care of Dad much like she did us children. Whenever he lost something, she'd know just where to look. He'd come in and want his meals at a certain time and everything done for him. She'd even pay the bills with the money he earned while trying to give us everything but himself. I especially remember how he used to try to show us he loved us with money. He really tried at Christmas, but the way he went about it was sending Mother to the store to pick things out for us. Then he would be just as surprised as we were when we opened our presents.

I didn't know until I was older that his expressions mirrored our own because at those moments he was getting to relive his own lost childhood, when he often didn't know what to expect. But as I became older, I also became angry as I realized that he never took the time or made the effort to buy something just for me. I think the first time he ever did was in my early 30s when, as I described in *The Flying Boy*, he gave me his father's pocket watch. Most of the times before, he thought money talked and said what he never could: "I love you." I could have lived without the money.

In my late teens I began using money much the same way. I began working for Dad when I was 11, so I always had more money than most of my friends (though when they'd be off knocking a ball around, I was knocking out parts in Dad's tool and die shop). I would tend to try to buy friendship and love much like my dad did. Dad would give people money or make them loans, thus many people thought he was a great guy. But he never learned to really give of himself, so he never had deep intimate friendships. Most men back then didn't, and most men don't today.

Many of the men I work with in my groups and work-shops are able to admit that. That's why they're there. Like most of their fathers, they can't get close to men, or maybe they have this one guy they can talk to who lives several states away. Fear of intimacy? You bet! And a lot of this comes from fearing Dad and just plain fearing masculinity as displayed by most of our dads or our cultural fathers and icons.

By the time I was 16, I would willingly spend more money than I had to try to impress people, especially women, trying, I'm sure, to buy their love. I remember in

my late teens, in one year alone I bought one sweetheart
an expensive coat, a ring, a stereo system and at one point
thought about buying her a car. And you know what?
During this time she was going with someone else. You'll
see this behavior repeated later in my story.

Those mornings Lucy and I spent in Austin were like
most of the nights — filled with unusual extraordinary
events. We were more like children with each other than
I'd ever been with anyone. And yet something about our
relationship was like two kids in their own backyard
trying to dig a hole to China.

One day we bought a big box of crayons and a Mandala
coloring book (a book of beautiful circular designs that
represent wholeness and completeness). At night we'd
color and talk; sometimes we colored them together and
sometimes separately. We were filling in the blank spaces
with shades and hues of innocence and experience as if
they were missing parts of us.

Very often in the morning and late evening hours, we
would dance in my dining room to Steve Winwood or
Marvin Gaye. Just the two of us . . . music blaring, hands
clapping and fingers snapping to rhythms that pulled us
out of the ordinary world. I had never done anything like
this before, and I don't think she had either.

The coloring, reading to each other, dancing, playing,
laughing were all golden threads that connected us. I
couldn't believe what was happening. A few mornings into
her visit she began to get present, and she knew it. Sitting
across from me at breakfast one morning she looked at me
and said, "You know, I love being with you. You make me
laugh and help me see the lighter side of things." No one
before had ever told me anything except how dark, serious
and intense I was and how I needed to lighten up.

Looking back, I can see that I had a tendency to be with women who were light and anything but intense. So I willingly and readily played Darth Vader. But I also realize that the darkness, seriousness and intensity came from a childhood that was anything but effervescent. It was very heavy.

For years I had to keep the pain to myself while carrying my mother's and father's. My own pain stayed buried in my face, laid heavy on my back, stuck in my shoulders and sickened my stomach. Much of the pain had been let go of by the time Lucy and I got together. I wanted to explore the lighter side for a change.

Yet I recall that the type of woman I was attracted to tended to be more attracted to the intense dark me and, indeed, to dark men in general. Sometimes I wonder if the phrase "tall, dark and handsome" has really nothing to do with skin tone, but rather darkness in a man's demeanor. Many women tell me in workshops that this is so. This darkness existing in many men is a signal and a warning sign that most women choose not to see. It's like a sign posted on their face: No trespassing, keep out of this heart. And many women love it because dark men need rescuing, fixing or taking care of, and they can pass this off as love. Many women long to take this wounded man, in whom they see so much potential, and love him out of his pain and heal his wounds. I call it the Florence Nightingale Syndrome. And, really, it's just a form of enabling the man to continue his patterns.

Once the dark man lets go of his pain by going into his wounds and feelings and releasing his emotions, lightness always comes. When it does, it scares him because he feels vulnerable. He's uncertain how to be without his cloak of darkness and his mask of intensity. Women then have little to rescue or fix. I had given up a lot of my darkness and was exploring a whole new mode of being. Lucy liked it at first. Now I realize she was pretty dark and intense herself. More on this later.

The days and nights of playing and dancing that first
week turned into two. By the last few days I felt that
Lucy was fully present. With each hour that brought us
nearer to saying goodbye, she became more vulnerable
and open. She still seemed unable to really feel her feelings about leaving. At this time I began to feel some old
feelings, too many and too familiar. I felt as if something
was being torn away from my body. Yet, due to the
newness of the relationship and considering how well
those two weeks went, I didn't fully experience this tearing until much later. I realize now that I didn't feel the
pull apart because I had not opened fully to her. I also
could still stay in my center and was maintaining my
personal power by keeping my tenuous boundaries intact,
at least for the moment.

So when we said goodbye, I basically felt okay. As
always, it took a couple of days before the separation fully
affected Lucy. Then the telephone calls that were ex-
changed and information traded made the New York stock
market seem dull in comparison. On the phone we told
secrets and sold each other shares in souls that had been
badly abused by our parents, our lovers and mostly ourselves. I would go to Mississippi again in less than a
month. If the telephones we talked through could talk,
they'd tell you the story of two people who loved but
couldn't say it, couldn't feel it and couldn't show it.

After my first book came out, my dad and I had an
incredible relationship over the phone. We went from
four years of not speaking to a deep healing. We went
from phone conversations that lasted less than two minutes and always ended with him saying, "I'm sure you
didn't call just to speak to me. Your mom is standing right
here, hold on. You can talk to her," to phone calls initiated
by him that lasted 20 to 30 minutes when we just talked
about things we had never discussed, ranging from the

simple to the sublime. We were really talking to each other for the first time. It felt great to be able to call my dad and just talk. He was present, open and honest and really there. I will always remember two calls I received from him right after *The Flying Boy* came out.

I sent him and Mom a copy of the book; I thought Mom would probably read it first and then either give a book report to Dad, who hadn't read a book of any kind since high school, or let him look at it and think about reading it, fearing what he might find. Instead the book arrived on a day that Mom was out of town. Dad, alone in their double-wide mobile home in the suburbs of Tampa, read it in one sitting. It so happened it was on the day I decided to call them to see if the book had actually arrived. Before I placed the call, I checked my answering machine and found one message containing only sounds of someone sobbing and then a click. I had no idea who it was and figured it must be a client trying to talk who couldn't for the tears. I checked my machine for the next call and again heard deep sobbing and a click. Still not knowing who had called, I called home later that evening and Dad answered the phone. As soon as I said hello, he broke into tears and I made the connection.

"Son, I read your book this afternoon." His voice was broken and cracked. "And I want you to know that it's true. Everything you said about me and your mother and my drinking is true. And, son, I'm proud of you. I'm real proud of you." Dad and I wept. We had (over the phone) managed to touch each other after wanting that touch for a long time. He and I could be as close as two people could possibly be . . . over the phone.

The second trip to Mississippi was tiring. I smiled to myself, though, as I thought of being with Lucy for four or five days. She had recently rented a beautiful rustic summer cottage overlooking a dark muddy creek. We had

known each other now for more than three months, had
been together six or eight times, and still had not made
love. I held onto the fact for comfort. I held onto it because
it told me this relationship was different from any I'd ever
had. We were putting the emphasis on being friends first
instead of me prioritizing my penis. I was so proud and yet
beginning to wonder when we'd become lovers.

As I arrived at the airport, my stomach became a little
queasy and my hands began sweating. I wasn't sure if this
was from fear of flying or fear of landing. Getting off the
plane, I started looking for her blue-brown eyes. At first
I couldn't see her. And when I did — I didn't. She had on
sunglasses and was reluctant to take them off. When she
did, we looked into each other's eyes, held each other
tightly, and I swear I felt I was holding air. She just was
not there. My heart sank as I had a familiar feeling.

When we say something is familiar about a person,
what we're really saying is that we're seeing, hearing or
feeling something that reminds us of someone in our
family of origin. When I have my groups meet, members
soon begin unconsciously to see their parents, siblings,
aunts and uncles right there in the group. Many see me as
a father, brother, sister or mother. When we are con-
sciously aware of this, there is no big problem.

When we're not aware of these transferences and pro-
jections, it can be devastating to any relationship, especially when we're emotionally upset, scared or afraid of
being abandoned or possessed. When this is the case, the
people we are in relationships with cease being who they
are and become who they remind us of. This restimulates
deep fears, anger, rage, confusion and other emotional
states. When this happens, we go into our fight-or-flight
mode. Either we start grabbing and holding on to people
and things, or we get the hell out of there.

Whatever our response, it becomes automatic, control-ling and ultimately very damaging because those people are not our parents or brothers or sisters. They probably don't even know them. And one thing I know for sure is that I desperately need to be seen for who I am, not what I do or who I remind someone of. Since I was seldom seen in my own family, I need my special loves to really see me. When they don't, I get angry and scared because it all feels so familiar.

Lucy and I talked tentatively and guardedly as we drove from the airport to the cabin. We couldn't be as open as we were in our phone calls. We couldn't be those people in the letters. We could only be adult children of alcoholics afraid of intimacy, abandonment, rejection and possession. So we chatted outside and shuttered inside and yet got along very well. All the while I felt she wasn't really there.

The cabin was moldy and musty but beautiful. Even in March it was warmer than I cared for, and the trees over-looking the brown river that crept slowly by reminded me of some primeval village where she and I had probably lived before. That at least was one explanation for why I felt I knew her so well. The real one would reveal itself later.

We unpacked the car and got comfortable in my quar-ters — a bedroom that she and I would share. After having fulfilled my mission (I thought at the time) of becoming friends, I knew I was ready for more. More was soon to come.

After we made love for the first time, something deep in me shifted. I have always heard women say that after they make love to a man, it's different and they can almost never return from that place. I realize now, since I feel I really have my own body back, that when I make love to someone I care about and intend to be with, we go into each other's blood and deeply into their spiritual body as well as their physical body.

As I recall with the lovers who I really cared for, particularly Laural, it took a long time to get them out of my
body once they left. And by getting them out, I only mean
enough to be able to comfortably be with someone else.
Now I know that you never really get them out, though
many people try as I have tried. I would use other women,
work, alcohol, whatever to try not to feel their mysterious
presence still moving through my cells, calling to me
through tissue and fiber, bone and muscle. The deep ones
are still there, no longer to be got rid of like a cancer, but
to be remembered and cherished as a part of me that will
always live beyond memory and time.

After Lucy and I entered each other for the first time,
we went downstairs, delighted, and colored in our Mandala coloring book and life seemed to be orderly and
dignified. And yet something was wrong. I walked out
and looked into the Mississippi night sky and banged my
head against it and stared at my empty hands and felt my
empty soul. I couldn't figure it out. There was something
wrong; something was missing. I'd felt that feeling thousands of times before and I always hoped that the hole
inside me would be filled, but it never was. I tried stuffing
the hole with work, worry, alcohol, sex, drugs, TV, but it
seemed I was doomed to be just like my dad.

At that moment I more fully understood the addict
looking for "the man" or the alcoholic looking through the
cupboards, finding only an empty bottle and then holding
it upside down. The last drop would touch a tongue that
refused to tell another just how much the hole in his soul
hurt. I was empty and I couldn't understand why, when
Lucy was just a smile away. She and I had just sexually
satisfied each other, and yet as I looked into the stars I
cursed their existence. They were closer to me than she
was, more available and reachable than she was. They
were even closer to me than I was to myself. I was always
very far away from myself except as a child.

One day I had a client bring to a session his pictures from childhood. He spread them out on the floor. He went through them, telling short stories about each, until he found one taken when he was about four years old. He looked at it as if he were seeing someone he used to know but had forgotten. And then the tears came. I said, "Bob, tell me about this little boy."

"He trusted. He dreamed. He felt everything was going to be all right." Then tears really came as he said, "Someone owes him an apology."

I remember the time I worked with my own pictures of childhood. Each picture up to a certain place in time captured this little boy who trusted, hoped and was just who he was. His smile was spread evenly across his face. His eyes gleamed like blue beads in a blue ocean. Then I arrived at this certain picture and the smile turned into an uneven snarl; the trust was gone and the dreams were drowned in wave after wave of whiskey, abuse and abandonment.

I went back into Lucy's house, sad, but committed to giving it some more time and seeing where this thing with her could go. I would wait and see if my needs could get met and the hole in me could get filled.

Waiting . . . Adult Children from dysfunctional families know how to wait. We don't have much patience, but we do know how to wait. We know how to wait for parents to stop drinking. We know how to wait for parents who are late to pick us up, we know how to wait on dates who nearly always run late for lunch and other appointments, or we know how to keep them waiting.

Now patience is something entirely different and is an animal very few of us have tamed or domesticated. We want to be fixed, well, healed and enlightened yesterday, or at the very most six weeks from now. We'll follow any guru, guide, quack, teacher or preacher who will promise instant recovery for the low, low price of a substantial donation of our money or our brains. But we know how to wait. We wait for husbands and wives, girl friends and boy friends to come back for years. Eventually perhaps we decide that, just because they're marrying someone else and having their baby, it doesn't mean they might not still be coming back.

We know how to wait on our partners in business and marriage to "change," but we have little patience with someone who is actively working on changing themselves and breaking old patterns. We have little patience for those who are less than perfect already — especially ourselves.

Lucy came to Austin a couple of weeks later and shared with me one of the most important days of my life — my first book-signing. So much of my life I had spent alone. Special occasions were seldom celebrated. Birthdays came and went without much notice. Christmas, New Year's, Thanksgiving were days spent alone in movie theaters because I tended to isolate and hide out when the rest of the world seemed to want company and family. I wanted it too, but I just couldn't admit it or ask for it. Every time I went home it seemed like a journey into deeper insanity. Even when friends would invite me to a turkey dinner, I'd always decline.

I secretly longed for the courage to go be around people who were comfortable with their families and could chat casually over dinner. For me dinner time was no pretty sight. Everyone ate as fast as they could, usually with one eye on the TV and the other on their own private escape routes. (Mine led to my bedroom or outside.) When it wasn't like that, it was every man for himself and Dad against all. He ruled over us like slaves who sneaked into the big house to pander a few crumbs. We ate well, but in a hurry and almost never happily.

So when Lucy made a special effort to be by my side that afternoon to wish me well and support me, it was like a break with the past. To tell the truth, I don't know that her being there with me didn't surpass the importance of the event itself. I knew this had to be love . . . What else could it be called? She was there. In many ways I think it was the first and last time she was fully there.

I know now how important it is for the one you love to be there for you and you there for them. I can feel how special that was for me, those moments signing autographs on a book that told the world just how little I was there for Laural, just how much she was there for me, and how her being there was unnoticed, unappreciated and abused.

You see, Mom and Dad were "there" for me growing up in some ways, but in the ways that really count they weren't. Dad was lost in liquor, Mom was lost in sickness and I was lost in the shuffle. So I never really learned how to be "there" for someone in a healthy way. I knew very little about being "there" for myself and not much about really being "there" for someone who loved me. I learned how to look like I was "there," but I was really somewhere else most of the time. I was in my head or just disassociated from what was going on outside of me. Yet I would try to be there for everyone who needed me. I was totally unable to form the word "no" on my lips. I would start to say the word "no" and "yes" came out every time. I could be tired, sick or just generally wanting, needing to be doing something else besides caretaking some friend by helping them move or listening to their life story for the thousandth time. But I would still say "yes." And since I couldn't really say "no" to people in need, I see now how very little my "yes" really meant.

Lucy was there. But being there for a lover seemed new for her, too, and I think it threw her into a deep place of fear and need to fly away. And she did. That evening at my large party (one of three in the last eight years) the woman who managed to be by my side during the day disappeared into the night and the past. She only popped back into the present now and then. And yet I thought very highly of her being there at all. One out of two, 50-50, one-half seemed like more than I deserved. It seemed like more than I ever got and more than I ever gave.

A few days later it was getting time for her to leave and go back to Mississippi. I knew I was falling in love with her and I was not addicted . . . yet. I looked her in the eyes over breakfast and something came out of my mouth that surprised and delighted both of us. The words had taken me three years to form before I was ready to place them in someone's ears. I was ready for a commitment.

"Lucy, I'm not going to put up with any bullshit. And I'm not going to give any out." Lucy sat over her oatmeal, stunned. "I'm not going to date other women and I need you to not date other men. And I'm not going to live with another woman before I marry you." If Lucy's teeth had been false, they would have fallen out.

"I hear you, and I respect you more than any man I've ever known," she said. I felt very strong, stronger than I'd ever been with any woman before. It would be only months later before I'd have to eat those words, along with several side orders of unspoken "no's."

So the days flew past. Lucy's visits went from days to weeks. She left right after the book-signing and returned about two weeks later. As usual, she got in late. As usual, she looked tired and tentative. I could tell that something was wrong but wasn't sure what, so I went into my caretaker routine. I tried to fix her by running her a bath, getting her something to eat and making sure I didn't appear angry at having been kept waiting again well beyond the time she said she'd arrive. Again, all this seemed so familiar.

I remember Mom taking care of Dad much like the fourth child she never had. She was always doing for him and seemed forever to be waiting on him. He'd always be later than he said he'd be. And then when he got home, usually very tired or drunk, she'd take care of him without ever expressing any anger. I think Mom was afraid if she didn't do all this she somehow would have failed as a woman. She seemed to get a lot of her self-worth from being able to play mother to Dad. I think she was also afraid that if she didn't take care of him, he'd go find someone who would. He probably wouldn't have, though he might. She saw her mother and nearly all the mothers of her generation do the same thing. And I saw my mother. That's where I learned it. I played out Dad's side of the pattern with my last love, Laural. And while I knew it was up to me to stop and learn new behaviors that worked, I first had to see and become aware of where I learned them.

Lucy slid into bed that night with the thought of lovemaking never entering her head. Me . . . I was more than ready after my three-week abstinence.

"Lucy, what's wrong?" I asked, knowing she didn't want to talk. "Nothing. I'm just tired and need to go to sleep." She was so very distant. I could tell she was somewhere else or had been somewhere else that wouldn't please me a damn bit. "Tell me. Are you seeing someone else?" Bingo, the losing number came up. I felt like hell as I saw the truth in her face.

"Yes. There's this guy in Mississippi that I met before I met you. We've been seeing each other for a while. But we're just friends, good friends. We have a lot in common, but I'm pretty sure it won't go anywhere. I think I should be with you if I'm going to be with anybody. I just have trouble with the idea of being with one man. And if I was going to be with one man, I think it would be with you."

I looked at her in disbelief and yet wanted and needed to trust her, knowing that something told me I shouldn't . . . couldn't. I wanted to more than anything in the world.

"Are you going to continue to see him? Because if you are, you're not going to see me."

"No, we'll just be friends."

"Are you sure?"

"Yes. I'll talk to him when I get back home. Now can we get some sleep? I'm awfully tired."

Good morning. I'm sitting looking out over the ocean, nestled in the mountains of Big Sur and letting the Esalen Institute shelter me from the real world. Esalen is a retreat on the California coast. My thoughts and feelings are elsewhere at the moment.

I am alone again. Even when I was with Lucy, I often felt alone, especially when she'd leave. Yet even though I'd feel lonely, it seemed as if I knew how to deal with these feelings much more effectively than I knew how to be with somebody and be in a "relationship."

Last night, eating in common with the Esalen work-shoppers, I felt so out of place, so noticeably different, like a two-headed man that everyone did not stare at out of politeness. I just plain didn't feel like I fit in. But that's been true my whole life; I just didn't fit in!

The way I tried to deal with this was to wear several masks: the mask of indifference ("I don't need anyone"), or the mask of self-sufficiency, the mask of darkness and intensity, the mask of the spiritually enlightened ("I don't need mere mortals or their frailties, failures or fatigue"), the mask of the intellectual ("I'm too damn educated to need anybody"). I had a trunk full of masks to make sure people didn't approach me because I knew more about being alone and dealing with the concurrent loneliness than I did about how to work with someone and how to be open. What if they left?

Consequently I was seen as a lone wolf, a master of disguise, a chameleon that changed to suit the moment, or the master who, out of some noble need to educate the masses, managed to stay on earth rather than ascend. And it was all bullshit!

The truth was that I was and still can be a control freak. I'm an adult child of an alcoholic who hates groups that I'm not in control of and am scared of people who might get my number and see through my disguises. Mostly, though, I'm a man who needs and wants to change the messages I send to myself, to open up to people and let them in, but it's so scary. I'm scared. I've been scared all my life. I got scared as a child. My alcoholic, dysfunctional family traumatized the shit out of me and I went into a state of chronic shock (*Chronic Shock* by Wayne Kritsberg) that I'm only now beginning to come out of. I'm not arrogant . . . I'm scared; I'm not enlightened . . . I'm lonely; I'm not self-sufficient . . . I need you. I'm just usually too scared to say so.

Over the years I've been able to say this to more and more people because I've dealt with much of the pain, relived the traumas and healed my wounds. But I still know more about being alone than I know about being with someone in a healthy functional way.

It was about this time, three months into love and addiction, that I decided Lucy and I needed a trip. I have always tended to think that a trip will accomplish all the things staying at home couldn't. It can tell if you're really compatible by decreasing the possible space between two people. It throws you into an intense state of awareness of each other's faults and flaws, and it guarantees intimacy of some kind. It also limits the possibility of abandonment, at least physical abandonment, especially if you pay for the trip and thus have most of the power.

I proposed the idea to Lucy. She was reluctant at first but she has always enjoyed traveling, adventurer that she is. "I don't have any money, John. I simply can't afford to go anywhere." Lucy spoke honestly.

"I tell you what, I'll pay for both of us. You don't need any money. Just say you'll go and we'll take a week off and go play and be together. This trip will be good for us. It will draw us closer. It'll be great. Say yes."

Luckily, in this case, Adult Children of Alcoholics usually can't say no, and no is the word addicts can't stand to hear. "Yes, I'll go. Thank you for the offer. Where shall we go?"

I knew how much she liked New Mexico, since she told me right after we met that she was thinking about living there. I loved the Santa Fe area as well. So we decided on Santa Fe and found a beautiful health resort just outside of the city. I called and made all the arrangements. In many ways I think this is where the sickness of the relationship really started. There were so many healthy things going on at the time that the "dis-ease" I was feeling about paying for the whole trip seemed like a necessary downside to get what I wanted — a week with a wonderful woman.

We got to Santa Fe, and Sunrise Springs was gorgeous. We checked in, awed by the countryside. We knew that we had made a smart choice.

We spent the first evening in delicious dining and soaking in hot tubs that looked out over the mountain guarded by a sky full of stars. Everything external was exceptional. Everything inside was as per usual. I longed for something I didn't have. I wanted Lucy to make the feeling of not having go away. Instead, Lucy went away, and when she didn't, I did. We seldom placed ourselves in the same moment at the same time, but when we did, we would be so together it scared us both. The anger at this started building in me. I wasn't getting what I was paying for or what I needed. The hotel was great, but the hope of intimacy was fading.

Lucy was half with me, half somewhere else about half the time. And yet I felt lucky to be with a woman of such charm who was so magical. But I had arranged it so I could feel used. After all, I was paying for everything. She was giving as much as anyone can who is scared to death of intimacy. I unknowingly had become a victim again, looking like a martyr, crying, "Beat me, beat me, make me write bad checks." And in the process was reminded of Mom and how she was with Dad.

I had to get out the anger that was building. I had done enough work on myself and with others to recognize that I was beginning to stuff it. I asked Lucy if she'd cooperate and do an exercise with me. She said she, too, was feeling angry but wasn't sure about what. I think she was mad at herself for being in the position to be the persecutor. I think she was also angry at me for carrying her financially, which usually creates resentment underneath, rather than gratitude.

We decided upon a process that would reduce the tension we felt. We went to our room and went to separate corners and threw pillows at each other as hard as we could. The room exploded with the energy that we had built up, as we thoroughly discharged it from our bodies. It allowed us to physically and symbolically show each other how angry we were without hurting ourselves or each other. When we finished, we both felt better, and then we talked about what was going on for each of us. It was great to be really talking. I immediately took this as a sign that we were really right for each other and that we could make it work.

Signs and omens are everywhere, and it seems I either don't notice them at all or I make them too important. The

other thing I tend to do is turn things into signs that
aren't. It's hard to not do the latter.

On the spiritual level I know that God speaks to us
through the physical world, particularly through plants,
animals and the stars. But I'll see television shows, or hear
songs on the radio, or see a car for the hundredth time
that day that reminds me of my ex-lover's car, and I'll
think these are signs that I should get in touch with them
or at the very least think about them for a while.

And then there are signs that really are signs but I don't
want them to be. For example, when I was dating Lucy I
could see that I had done all I was doing with her before,
with another person. It was when I was 16 to 21. I loved
this other unavailable woman so much. I was devoted to
her and devoured her attention (when it came) like a
banquet the hungry seldom get to see, let alone eat. She
dated others while I pledged my unwavering love and
loyalty to her. The only thing she ever pledged was loyalty
to the sorority she belonged to in college. And yet I
bought her coats, a stereo, jewelry, helped her get a job
where I worked and watched her leave the store with
other men. I was angry about as much as I was in love. I
wanted only her and she took whatever I'd give.

Now here's where the signs came in. On two separate
occasions with Lucy I was feeling taken for granted and
victimized and knew that I had been there before but I
didn't want to believe it. I needed not to believe it; I was in
denial. On my way to dinner with Lucy, whose meal I
intended to pay for gladly again, I saw a 1969 black
Toronado, the exact kind of car my old girl friend had
from the ages of 18 to 20. The minute I saw it I couldn't
help but say to myself, "You're doing it all again. You're
repeating past mistakes." As soon as I said that to myself,
I thought, "Okay. There's almost no way this could be a
sign. There must be at least five black 1969 Toronados
still around in the U.S., even though to that day I had seen
only one of them. It's just a coincidence and doesn't mean
anything. Forget it. It's just a car."

Lucy and I got to the restaurant. We were sitting by the window, she somewhere else, me looking out the window, waiting to order, wondering why I felt the way I did, when a candy-apple red Corvair convertible pulled up and parked right in front of me. It was the exact same kind and color of car that the same girl friend of the past traded in for the black Toronado. And you know, I still didn't see the connection. The signs were there, but I didn't want to see any of them. By the fourth month of the relationship the signs were posted in such large letters a blind man could have seen them. But not a man blinded by love, need and addiction.

There's an old Buddhist saying: Before enlightenment a mountain is a mountain. During the process of enlightenment a mountain is something else. After enlightenment a mountain again becomes just a mountain.

During the next few weeks Lucy and I moved in and out of intimacy like two kids trying to enter a cold water bath or water too hot to touch. But there was so much good stuff that I wanted to believe she was the one.

One night she and I were arguing about some insignificant something and I got up, put on a pair of shorts, and stomped to the front porch. I looked into the darkness and then at the pattern that I was living out.

I thought to myself, "My God, how many times have you been right here before?" The answer was, "hundreds." I thought, "It's time to break some old patterns and see what happens."

My pattern is to leave. According to my pattern I would go back in the house, get dressed, tell whoever was lying in the dark that I was going for a drive and come back in several hours and stuff whatever emotions might be trying to surface. At that moment I ran the pattern through my mind's eye. I decided to do something immediately, anything as long as it was different. So I got up and moved past the fears and went back to bed and said, "Please hold me." And Lucy did, and I cried and told her I was hurting. The next morning I felt like I'd punched a hole in a life-long pattern that had ruled me. She then felt free enough to break into tears herself and asked me to hold her as she went into her own painful place. We came close and we managed to tear down some walls.

Breaking patterns is hard. First they have to be identi-fied, but identification won't break them. We have to not only see what they are but what we get out of them. There is no pattern that we've ever adopted that does not get us something. When it no longer serves us, we stop doing it. First we name it, then see where it came from, what it gets us and then go against it. Sounds easy, doesn't it? Well, we all know it's not easy. Here's one reason why.

I asked a client of mine who was describing the patterns he and his wife have around intimacy, "Richard, what do you get out of those patterns?"

"Nothing but pain," responded Richard.

"Bullshit, you get something or you wouldn't do them," I responded. Richard looked at me, surprised at my lan-guage or my readiness to confront him. "I don't get any-thing but the same old thing."

"Bingo!" I said. "The same old thing. Listen to what you're saying."

I asked Richard to tell me how the pattern performs its magic. In a nutshell what he said was this: "She'll do this and I'll do this, and then she'll do this and I'll wait a few days and say this, and then she'll respond and then every-thing will be okay until next time."

What Richard said for all of us who rely on patterns is that as long as we let them run us, we know exactly how things are going to turn out . . . the same way they always do. Knowing how this will turn out is worth so much to the many of us who are control freaks. It gives us a sense of order, even if it hurts like hell. Most of us prefer the known to the unknown, and any time we try to go against or break a pattern, we plunge headlong into the unknown where all kinds of things await us. That's scary, so we stay with the familiar, even though it cripples us in relationships.

When I got up and went from the porch and out of the pattern, I made a journey into the mystery, into the magic of the moment, and I was terrified. Would Lucy reject me? Laugh at me? Leave me? Love me?

A long time ago a particular response to a particular situation worked for us, saved us and allowed us to survive something. Responses are usually only good for one event, but we turn them into patterns that almost never work the way they did the first time.

Each time we go against a pattern that has shielded us from the raw opportunities of the moment, we create an opportunity for change for all those involved. If I stop doing what I've always been counted on by others to do, they have to stop what they've always done as well. If I shift, the other person has no one to bounce off of. Thus they are left either to discover something else to do or go find someone else that will enable them to play out their ancient pattern. And many of us are deathly afraid that they'll do just that: leave us and go find someone else who will match their patterns the way one or both of their parents did.

Relaxed by the cool air and enhanced by the mountains and sunsets, we left Santa Fe. On the way home we created games that I'd never played with anyone before, healing communication exercises.

While in the airport we pretended that we'd just met each other and we would tell each other about our last relationship (the last one being the one we were now

having). We would share what was good about it and what
was not so good, but not what the other person did or
didn't do, talking only about ourselves as much as possible.

While I can't remember everything she told me or
everything I told her, I do remember that exercise described her patterns of unavailability, fear of intimacy
and inability to be with just one man. I listened but didn't
want to hear. I couldn't hear because my ears were
stuffed with my own stuff.

The next exercise I would recommend to anyone. We
pretended the other person was our best friend, and we
told them about each other as if our friend did not know
or had not even met our lover. Lucy went first, pretending
I was an old friend from school she had not seen in a long
time. She told me (now playing the role of her friend who
also could ask questions) about myself for 45 minutes.
She described me in terms and ways that touched and
moved me deeply. I could really hear how much she cared,
what she valued about me and what she saw that I didn't
even know was visible. It was truly a moving, enriching
experience. I proceeded to do the same, pretending I was
telling Caleb, a friend in Florida, about Lucy. I'll never
forget those moments.

Such moments had never happened with a woman before. I never knew how Laural really felt about me until it
was way too late. We had loved and hated each other for
years and I thought I knew how she felt about me, but it
wasn't the way she honestly felt about me. One day, right
before my book came out, we met and talked. We were
not communicating very well, as usual, when suddenly
she said, "Why are you so scared of me?" I said, "Because
I know how you feel about me and think about me."

"How do you think I feel about you?" she said with a
serious look on her face. I started crying, "Laural, you
don't value me or like me much." I stopped crying and
turned to her.

She took my face in her hands and looked me in the
eyes. "John, I love you and I respect you very much. I
respect your work, the way you love and care for people,

and the way you try to help them. You're a good man, an honest man, a smart man." Laural went on for several minutes, telling me things and feelings about me that I never even knew about before. I was crying buckets by this time. I had no idea that she saw me as anything but evil and anything but one more big disappointment in her life. But it was too late. I wish I had known earlier, but at least I heard it.

Years later I realized that what Laural told me that day was what I had always wanted to hear from my father. I was always afraid of her, much as I was of him. Since she never said these things directly to me, I guess I confused the two and made her into him. She wasn't. She was Laural, who loved and respected me just as I was. She loved me unconditionally all those years.

The Middle

Lucy and I went home and began the period of our demise, although I wouldn't admit it until much later. Lucy couldn't give up her Mississippi man. She tried and she tried. She also tried to convince me time and time again that she knew in her head I was the right man for her. Each time we got together, I could tell that she had been with him and couldn't really be with me. It always took several days before she could get semi-present, and her availability always increased about the time she was ready to leave. Once safe at home two states away, she'd call and be as close and intimate as anyone could be. The pattern was repeated over and over again. I'd act as if I were getting what I needed. I thought all I had to do was wait, and she'd see it was me she loved.

About four months into the relationship Lucy began thinking about moving back to Austin, and I really tried to reinforce those thoughts. I'm sure now she didn't really want to come back. It had taken so much courage to leave Austin earlier for the place she really wanted to be. I'm guessing here, but I'm pretty sure she thought about leaving her Delta home to be with me. And I guess that was as much to do with her trying to find a way to get away from the man there (a man she knew she couldn't be with) as it was to be with me. But the bottom line was that she was willing to compromise herself and what she really needed. Now, on the surface, that may appear to be a step in the right direction, but it wasn't. It was a step deeper into something else.

I think everything would have been far worse if I had not started doing one thing long before Lucy started telling me about moving back to Austin: letting go. It's something I'd started learning, been forced to learn after Laural left a few years ago. I'm still not very good at it. But that first weekend I spent with Lucy once again showed me the necessity of turning loose the one you love. Though I did not know it at the time, I was practicing detaching, a word I would not use until months later. It was a process I was certainly unable to do before I did all the work I described in my first book.

I began letting Lucy go after each encounter, each disappointment and each disappearance. This detaching allowed me to hurt less and allowed her to feel safe enough to come back to me again and again and open up to me at deeper levels. I couldn't always detach. As a matter of fact, my fear of abandonment was so great at times I would clamp down on her like a pair of Vise-Grips and cling to her for dear life.

Mostly I found that the more I could let go and let God have the situation, the better I felt and so did she. So I just kept giving her and the relationship over to God again and again. But, you know, deep down inside I knew I had no choice. Even the control freak that I am, I knew I did not make this thing happen, was not in control of her any more than I controlled Texas weather. I just wanted to believe I was in control, and when I did, it was always a disaster. I kept working on detaching and letting go and still loving.

In my family of origin I never saw much letting go or detaching. What I saw was someone, my dad or mom, threatening to leave or trying to control the other through threats, manipulation and domination. My mom's love was off the mark as much as my alcoholic father's. Neither could let go of the other or us children. She was unconsciously dependent on him and his drinking. She got things from him which she didn't think she could live without. He took care of her financially, .and she got to take care of him physically, emotionally and spiritually and in the process appear to be the long-suffering devoted wife.

Mom could not let go of Dad and detach and Dad couldn't let go of Mom. Neither could hear their still small inner voice that must have whispered, perhaps screamed that they should love each other enough to set the other free. Instead, they clung to each other out of desperation, rather than loving devotion. Mom, who never learned to swim, clung to Dad like a life preserver in a sea made of tears, but the life preserver offered little buoyancy.

Somewhere, somehow, in spite of all of this I learned to listen to that voice inside me. Not all the time, but a good portion of the time. I could trust that voice to guide me the way it did when, as I recounted in *The Flying Boy*, it told me to go to the place where I would meet Laural.

When Laural and I first parted, now over four years ago, I asked her why she was leaving. "John, you didn't love me the way I needed. And you didn't teach me a whole lot. But one thing you did do. By listening to your own inner voice, you showed me that I must listen to my own. For that I thank you."

"What did your inner voice tell you to do?" I asked, already knowing the answer. "It said I had to leave you."

"That inner voice," I said with a smile, because I was happy for her and glad she got something from me besides pain, "that inner voice — you can't go around trusting just any old inner voice. Who told you that stuff? Your real inner voice would say, 'Stay, Stay, Stay!'"

We both laughed for the first time in months. "Well, if your voice said go, I guess that's what you'd better do. You think you'll ever come back?" Tears began falling. "I will if my inner voice tells me to." She hugged me and I knew then she was gone, though it would take years to accept.

She loved herself and me enough to let go. I've been trying to learn how for a long time. But I began practicing with Lucy and I did fairly well.

One of the ways I did this was to begin grieving and releasing the sadness and anger around what I already knew to be an ill-fated future for us as a couple. After she'd go back to Mississippi or I'd leave her there, I'd usually spend quite a bit of time in tears. When I got to somewhere safe, I would scream and yell and pound out my anger. It was in this form of letting go I could release her more honestly and deeply.

But a curious thing always happened for a while. The more I'd let her go, the more she could and would be there. I see now that when someone fears intimacy, possession and abandonment, the more room they have, the more comfortable and safe they feel to be with another. When I'd get scared that Lucy was leaving, I'd grab on and hold on. The result would be her feeling forced to leave. It seems the very thing we're afraid of the most is the thing that is guaranteed to happen, since most of our actions are directed and patterned to get the results we say we don't want. I didn't want Laural or Lucy to leave, and yet leaving was what I had always known. Staying I didn't know and didn't trust. I only knew how to be alone. The truth is that clinging and holding onto anything in life is just the opposite of what life demands — letting go. I really started my training with a woman who was as hard to hold as the wind.

Lucy and I began putting our heads together to try to figure out how she could support herself in Austin. She had worked in a bookstore and was a most talented potter, but neither separately could provide a good living. Once again, aging errant knight that I am, I whistled for my white horse, mounted him, and told Lucy she could work for me. My counseling practice was going great, my book was selling well and I was getting offers to lecture and do workshops around the country. I asked her to work for me as my partner and assistant. I promised good pay and great fringe benefits . . . I'd be her un-health insurance if she'd take care of her own and my social insecurity. I don't know how she really felt about the idea, but she accepted the offer. I felt great because she would really be with me and terrible because I had just stepped back into a pattern of rescuer and caretaker one more time.

She started working, setting up radio and television interviews, typing, etc. Just when I thought I had her, she came out with the words, "John, I can't move back to Austin."

She told me that she still had her life in the swamps of Mississippi and needed to be there longer to discover the mysteries of her past. Her Indian heritage was still needing to be discovered. And I, one who misses to this day his home in the hills of Alabama, understood. She took a box of my media paraphernalia back to Mississippi, swearing to continue to work for me from there, and we could continue our long-distance romance and current business relationship. She was gone again.

The next thing I did was start thinking . . . maybe it's time to leave Austin and move back southeast, like, say, to Mississippi. I would give up one of the most successful things I'd ever done, my friends, clients, a great house and start over again from scratch. I was thinking about giving up everything to be with her.

"Lucy, what would you think if I said I'd be willing to live in Mississippi?" I asked early one morning in May.

"Move here?" Her voice sounded desperate and scared. "What would you do here?"

"I don't know. Maybe open a counseling practice, or try to get a teaching job."

"But your whole life right now is in Austin. Things couldn't be better for you there."

I began to sense that Lucy wasn't exactly behind the idea.

We talked about me moving there several times before I came to my senses and saw that the thought of me moving scared the hell out of me and her. It wasn't a good idea to traumatize either of us to such a degree.

We moved a lot as a kid. My dad, like many men and women, wanted to believe moving was the answer to his problems. He was one who believed deeply in geographical cures. Dad and Mom moved from the hills of Alabama to the suburban streets of Detroit, Michigan. After years of struggling to make ends meet, they decided to pack us up and move back to Alabama and struggle to make ends meet. They thought it easier to scratch out a living among their kin and kind.

That first move to Alabama tore me up and traumatized me to degrees I still can't come to terms with. I had to say goodbye, not only to my best friends, but to a way of life as well, the only one I knew. It was marked by better education, racial integration and a Northern orderliness that would not appear in the South until many years later (and in some parts not even yet). It was replaced by the uncertainty of one move after another. Until I was 13, we moved so many times I can't count them. I was in and out of schools that were segregated, without art and music classes, trying to become friends with kids who hated "Yankees" and "Niggers" or anyone different than they.

The hardest part was not having friends and yet always having to try to make them in those new places, just in case Dad decided to stay put.

I remember one time moving from one city to another and back in the span of six weeks. And, you know, no one ever explained it to me, much less apologized, but I sure was hurt by that. Moving is harder on children than most adults will ever know, mostly because they live with the illusion that kids are so flexible and that they'll adapt. But moving is one of the most stressful things in an adult's or child's life. If not done in a sensitive way with lots of communication of feelings, it can be devastating.

It only took a few days for me to come out of my mini-blackout and begin thinking clearly again. I couldn't move to Mississippi. If I did, it would only be because I was afraid of losing Lucy. I didn't want to go there because it was the highest good for me; it was a way of trying to capture her. We talked over the phone for hours about the awkwardness of a long-distance relationship. We both were semi-aware of how safe the miles made us and at the same time how lonely. The distance left us free to fantasize and keep the "perfect partner" in our heads. But the truth for me was that I was really learning to love this phantom.

The spring brought Lucy to stay with me for about a month, and that sheer amount of contact brought up all kinds of fears. One evening after a full day of work, wrestling with the destructive patterns of those who came to see me in counseling, my own demons from childhood began to want out and I needed to give some old wounds some attention. Lucy and I crawled into bed. I was tired and I began crying. I'd stop and then begin again. I was going into what has been called by some a spontaneous rebirthing, or what Arthur Janov and I refer to as a spontaneous primal. Whatever you call it, it is a return to a deep place of hurt and woundedness that is as old as I and as old as man.

I was afraid for Lucy to see me this way — vulnerable, open, scared and deeply in pain. My own body began trembling and convulsing slightly. At the time while I knew that this was healthy and normal, I also didn't know what it was really all about. I did know I was afraid to be seen this way by any woman who I loved as much as I loved her.

"John what's wrong?" Lucy looked at me in a way that told me she wasn't afraid.

"I'm just sad."

"Sad about what?" she said, as she slid closer to me.

"Sad about everything. You. Me. The pain my clients carry. I'm still sad about Laural and the pain we caused each other."

"You can let it out, John. It's okay. Honest. I'll stay with you."

"Mostly, I'm sad because I'm afraid I can't trust you to see me this way." I began crying deeply and shaking more and more.

Finally, I remembered that I had been here before. I started crying from a place so deep inside me that it is seldom felt. I put a pillow over my mouth and a scream came out that symbolized and vocalized the pain I was still feeling around some unresolved childhood hurts. Lucy held me, and for about 30 minutes I wasn't alone. I let her see me and yet didn't need her to be responsible for my pain nor need her to fix me.

After that I thought to myself, "This woman understands, and if she doesn't leave, I won't have to be alone anymore." She showed me the next morning just how much she understood.

The sun came up and Lucy went down into her own pain. She woke up crying. Like me, at first she was afraid to show it. Like me, she knew how much she needed to. I could see what was happening. My openness the night before brought up stuff for her and also gave her permission to do the same if she needed to. She didn't feel completely safe, but after a few words of encouragement and two arms (made stronger from the night before) placed firmly around her, she cried and screamed and hurt and let it out and cried and screamed some more.

We were close, perhaps closer in some ways than we'd ever been with anyone. We understood each other. And I hoped and wanted to believe this would be the person . . . "the One." I began making plans to capture this will-o'-the-wisp of a woman. I was going to ask her to marry me.

At this time I had an incredible dream that told me exactly what to do. In the dream I was driving a team of mules, but we weren't going anywhere. Two of Lucy's teachers appeared. Both were older women who have passed on much knowledge and wisdom to Lucy in the last several years. The women were dressed in full-length dresses, the kind Southern women wore in the field years ago. They came up to me and pointed out that I had the reins wrapped tightly around the back wagon wheel, hence the mules could not go forward. They unwrapped them and one simply instructed me to hold the reins loosely. It was that same day I had said to Lucy, "You're as stubborn as a mule."

She had been with me the whole month of May. Lucy and I finally relaxed into each other in a way we hadn't before. I remember one night we were lying on my couch watching TV. There was a smile on her face . . . one of contentment and peace. She looked at me and her face lit up and her whole body spoke the words: "This is not bad."

I still was not fully in touch with the fact that my needs were going unmet and how much I was trying — no, striving — to meet hers. I wanted her. I needed her.

The next night we decided to go see a psychic, one that I had visited a year before and had a lot of confidence in because so much of what she said would happen, did. Lucy had visited psychics before, so she was relaxed and receptive.

We entered the psychic's home and listened as she read our cards. We wrote down everything she said.

"There will be a brown-haired woman try to come between you and Lucy, John," she said in her Spanish accent. "And there will be a blond-haired man in your life

that will come between you and John." Lucy and I looked
at each other. I thought I knew who the woman was or
who I was hoping it would be. Lucy sat silently staring
into the distance.

The psychic, sitting in her leather chair, surrounded by
her cards and in an atmosphere of mystery, said, "But you
will be married within one year and have three children
and be very happy with each other. Lucy, you will assist
John like a secretary or a partner in his business."

We both looked at each other, since we had just talked
that day about her entering more fully into my profes-
sional career. But the words that stung me like giant bees
were ". . . and you will be married within one year."

Lucy and I left the psychic's house with smiles and some
trepidation. She was as far away as the North Pole. But I
knew what was coming next. If I could bring her close
enough, long enough, I'd ask her a most important question.

Psychics have become increasingly popular and placed
in high demand lately. Adult children trying to cope in
an ever-changing world as they carry the memory of
their chaotic childhood deep within them, readily turn to
psychic phenomena. We look for answers to the same
questions generations before us had to answer, but we
have more tools and more spendable income than our
parents. We ask healers, teachers, gurus and guides.
Some are genuine, some are hucksters daring to disguise
themselves as helpers. Some are not unlike the false tent
preachers preaching salvation in the '30s and '40s (and
today, come to think of it), many of whom were about as
"saved" as my cat.

There are some psychic people. Indeed, most of us
have vast untapped psychic abilities ourselves. But there
are many would-be psychics who failed at computers,
accounting or psychology and who now serve the public

a slice of their own special, sometime harmful brand of neurosis. At least it borders on neurosis to believe that you can accurately tell your patron what the future holds in store.

As an adult child of an alcoholic, I have found myself at times so unsure of my direction, my needs, my goals and my partners that I have sought out psychics to point the way. I have asked them to give answers that I know only lie within and only time can yield. I have depended on them to make the pain of not knowing more bearable. While there are genuine psychics out there, and I've visited one or two, most are preying upon the vulnerabilities and insecurities of people who will pay almost any amount to know if the person they love will stay, leave or come back. And you and I already know for a fact some people stay, some leave, some come back. But few, very few "psychics'" know any more about the whos and whens than does the person asking the questions, hurting inside and scared to death of the answer.

With the words of the psychic, "you will be married," ringing in my ears, Lucy and I left and went for coffee and dessert. On the way I asked her, "Do you think she's right?"

"Right about what?"

"You know, about us getting married." I was a little scared. We had never used the "M" word before.

"Yes. I think she's probably right. It makes sense to me," Lucy said straightforwardly.

"You do?" was all I could say.

The next night after a delicious dinner at the Clarksville Cafe, I asked the scariest question for only the second time in my 35 years of life. The first time was a few years before to Laural, after she was too long gone to say anything but no.

It took all the courage I could find to form the words. The cafe was dark. The sounds of glass and silverware and people dropped out of existence for a brief instant. For one moment in time we two were all that existed. I looked into her eyes.

"I think we ought to get married. What I mean is, will you marry me, Lucy?" Like water the words washed over her. She wasn't afraid, but she wasn't answering either. She looked at me and finally she said, "Probably." She smiled. "Thank you for asking me to marry you. Thank you so much. Do I have to answer you right now?" She looked shy, pleased and proud.

"No, you can take some time."

"I'll take only a short amount of time and I'll think about it and tell you my answer soon. I'm really touched with your tenderness and caring enough to ask me."

We left the restaurant holding hands, went home and made love and officially entered the beginning of the end.

"Probably" was like "maybe," which is like "wait and see," which to an adult child of an alcoholic usually is heard as, "no." It seemed that whenever an important question was asked in my family, I seldom got a straight answer. I got put on hold for days, a week or forever. I think that's one reason I hate it so much when I call someone important and I get this businesslike voice that says even before you can answer, "Can I put you on hold?" The "maybes" in my family usually meant "no." My dad had very little time for me so I got "nos" from him on a regular basis.

I read a study the other day that said the average child between the ages of two and six hears the word "no" 85 times for every one "yes." I began thinking that, if this is so, it's no wonder adult children from dysfunctional families hate the word "no" so much that they almost totally exclude it from their own vocabulary. We heard the word so much we decided never to use it if possible and, therefore, in one less way sound or be like our parents.

Most adult children just don't know how to use the word "no" except to themselves. "No, I can't have this." "No, I don't deserve to rest." "No, I don't have the time to eat a good meal." Etc., etc. etc.

Lucy went back to Mississippi, and I sat on her "probably" like a mother chicken on an egg that I hoped with patience would hatch into a "yes."

For a couple of weeks, I in my nest of waiting and Lucy in the arms of another man (though I really didn't know this at the time) wrestled with the question I'd asked. Finally, she called me.

"John, before I can say yes, I think it would be a good idea if you come to Mississippi and spend some time here. You could visit my friends and get to know them, get to see me with them and how I am here. After that, we can talk about marriage. I need to stay here for a while longer and I need to be with you here before I can answer. What do you think about that?"

Without so much as a blink, without the thought entering my mind to even say, "Let me think about it," I said, "yes."

So I went to Mississippi in search of love and family. Lucy's friends and family, while frightening, would be familiar. They were at the very least fellow Southerners.

I decided to spend time in Lucy's land. I would see how she was there and see if I could fit in. I never really felt I fit in anywhere, but I'd give it a try. I'd transformed myself to fit any situation many times before. Surely I could do it again without exhausting my chameleon-like abilities.

Trying to fit in, wearing a mask, changing like the chameleon . . . these were what I knew. I never felt I fit in. While I prided myself on the fact that I could meet and talk to anyone from any walk of life (like my father), no matter where I went I always felt like fleeing for not feeling I fit in. In high school I wasn't a jock, a brain or a stud. I wasn't ever quite in but not ever quite out. I had friends in each group, from each socio-economic level, and yet never felt connected to any group in particular. It was the same in college and later in adult life. I wasn't like the other teachers or counselors that I knew. It seemed I was alone and yet could adapt my behavior to fit almost any situation for a short while. Master of disguise, I slipped in and out of roles and masks like one actor playing all the parts in an improvisational play. The play produced a product rather than a person. I never knew who I really was and where I really belonged. I felt unique and different and alone and that no one else was like me or would ever know what I was talking about.

I've noticed these same feelings come up for others many times in my groups and workshops for adult children from dysfunctional families. They all come in with this face on. This face that they wear in public that smiles a lot even when they're hurting. They look in control and together and ready to say yes or whatever they feel the other person wants them to say. Because we care so much about what others think and feel, we present our *persona* (the Greek word meaning mask) and continue the play even in a workshop or group. With time and safety, I watch my group members descend into their bodies, their wounds and pain. The tears, the grief and the anger come, and right before our very eyes they get back the face they were born with. After a good, deep cry or scream or burst of anger their face is retrieved from the past. They go into themselves and find their own fire that burns brightly and deeply within them, and like Prometheus, they bring it up and out for themselves and humankind. It is their face . . . not the face their mother or father or teacher needed to see. But it is one temporarily free of stress, darkness and intensity. Their light shines for a while and can shine for longer and longer amounts of time as more of the woundedness is experienced and released. The mask is peeled off, not without pain, but the process is less painful than keeping it on and keeping everyone out.

Lucy took me to all her special places and introduced me to her special people. Two older women, both Lucy's mentors, teachers and friends, seemed to like me well enough. I enjoyed their company as well. Margaret, the woman Lucy saw as a best friend and confidante even though she was much older, appeared very wise to me. I especially liked her, and several months later she would be my nocturnal mentor in another important dream that I would disregard for over a year.

After a few days I settled into the slow pace that has been constant in the deep South. I looked at the land and the river, and with the exception of the moss that hung lazily off tall trees, it reminded me a lot of Alabama. The "How ya'alls" rang in my ears like the "welcome home" would if I ever returned to the hills of Alabama and Tennessee.

So, needless to say, I began doing some serious fantasizing and began telling my daydreams out loud to Lucy. "What would you think if I said let's get a small house here and stay most of the summer and yet keep my house in Austin?"

Lucy looked at me with disbelief. She was scared, delighted and off the hook to give me an answer about marriage or moving back to Austin.

"You . . . move . . . here . . .?" Lucy spoke the words like television Indians did back in the '50s.

"Yeah. We can get a place, fix it up. It'll be great. We can take some time. Really see each other and then at the end of the summer you can answer my question. What do you think?"

Lucy, still stunned, said, "Let me think about it for a while." We went to the best catfish place in town and discussed the pros and cons over dinner. We decided to boldly go where Lucy and I had not gone in many years . . . into the land of living together.

Remember my pronouncement a few months ago? "I won't live with another woman until I marry her."

"Boundary . . . all . . . gone," said the child, just learning to talk, to someone who asked, "Where is your boundary?"

Adult children from dysfunctional families don't really know much about boundaries. They know how to leave, fly away or "glom" onto and enmesh, but not how to establish and maintain boundaries. The ones we had as children were often trampled on and crossed on a regular basis. Our parents knew as little about boundaries as we do.

Mom was forever saying what she wouldn't do, only to find herself doing it days or weeks later. Dad's boundaries were blurred by alcohol and the belief that men had the inalienable right to cross any boundaries they wanted to, especially women's.

Mostly it seems that many adult children have boundaries made of Velcro. That's why when adult children go through any form of separation you hear this tearing, peeling noise, and then you see them attach themselves as soon as possible to someone else.

Boundaries . . . still a hard concept for me to grasp, but I know they can and must be established if one is to be healthy in a relationship to oneself or another.

After a couple of disappointing days of searching for just the right love nest, we finally found a place we could afford. Or I should say, as it turned out, that *I* could afford. The house was large and roomy and on a tree-lined street close to the only health food restaurant in town and within walking distance of the huge park and small college. We had the back three rooms that had been turned into a comfortable studio for a struggling artist, old person or adult children of alcoholics who were unable to achieve intimacy and willing to settle for intensity.

After much debate and discussion we decided to take it. And on "our" back steps Lucy broke out a bottle of cola. Shaping paper cups into paper hats we toasted ourselves, our courage and our new home.

The next day I paid the rent and the utility deposits with the promise Lucy would pay her share later. We jumped into her station wagon and drove back to Austin to get some of her things she had in storage in my garage. The next day I rented her a U-Haul and bought a trailer hitch to attach permanently to her car. We loaded it up with a kiss and a promise that I'd be there in ten days. She was off — I mean gone.

The hours passed like months, the fear rose like flood waters. I tried not to think about what we were doing and needed to believe that the uncertainty was normal. But I was afraid. Lucy had a history of being a Houdini, a master of escape, a disappearing virtuoso, an adult child of an alcoholic scared to death of commitment . . . a Flying Girl. I thought if this isn't Karma, I don't know what is.

I must have called her every night, trying to minimize the panic that made my voice go an octave higher as we talked. Finally, about 24 hours before I was to leave for Mississippi to be with the woman I loved, I began to have second thoughts about the whole thing and needed to express them to her.

The phone rang a dozen times or maybe four times but it seemed like a long time before she answered.

"Hello," Lucy said in her most happy voice.

"Hi! How you doing?"

"Great. The house is really coming together nicely. I think we made a good choice and I'm glad you're coming. I think you'll enjoy spending time here. How are you doing?"

"Well, to tell you the truth, I'm not doing real well." I paused and thought about covering up my fear because of how it might bring her down to make her fearful. She sounded so clear and eager and really the most present I could remember her ever being.

"I'm having second thoughts about what we're doing. I'm not sure I'm really ready to move in and I'm having a hard time trusting you on this. My head says one thing and my gut says go . . . run away . . . leave. Don't move in."

"John, listen, give it a chance. It's going to be okay. It's going to work. Every day I'm moving more and more in the direction that you want. I'm getting excited and comfortable with the possibility of us getting together and making everything work out." She sounded so sure of herself.

"Lucy, I just don't know. You sound great. You sound happy and pretty certain we've done the right thing. I just don't know about it all."

Lucy got quiet for a moment and then with gentleness in her voice said, "John, don't make any decisions about this until you get here and we can talk. Promise me you'll come and not decide until you're here and we can talk face to face. Promise."

I took a deep breath and the words came out. "Okay. I promise. I'll not make any decisions about this until I get there tomorrow and we can talk. You will be there to meet my flight then?"

"Yes. I can't wait to see you. Now don't forget you promised. Don't worry. It's going to be all right. I am moving in your direction daily. Goodbye. I'll see you Friday morning."

Up at five-thirty, plane left at six-thirty, arrived Mississippi at eight o'clock. I was nervous, scared, excited and yet there was some sense that all this was just too good to be true. Too many things were working out too well. I couldn't help but think there weren't enough shoes hitting the floor. I was waiting for the other one to drop. Waiting for Trouble, like an old troll, to come out from underneath the bridge and get me. I didn't know what was wrong, so I kept telling my body to relax and telling my inner voice to shut up, that everything would be just fine.

The body has a wisdom and voice of its own. I had spent years getting back in touch with my body and learning to take the voice seriously. Put a woman I want in the picture and all this would go out the window. Tight shoulders, aching lower back, knots in the stomach, tense vocal chords and buttocks, shallow breathing, pounding heart are all signals that something is wrong. They tell us we're not feeling safe, that we're scared, angry, something . . . but they are there to be listened to, not ignored or medicated away. It is the body that signals the mind, and when we are in distress, the mind cannot think clearly. It is the body that tells us when we're in co-dependency. Since so many of us are afraid to listen to our bodies, we fly up into our heads and find the switch that reads *OFF*, throw it and just turn the body off like a thing the mind was meant to control.

The lower back begins to ache, and rather than listening, we take aspirins, caffeine or a drink and disregard it and go on. The stomach aches, we eat antacids by the bottle, tell it to shut up and go on. It's as if we think we are our heads. We tell our bodies to take us to work or play or into sex, then we experience disease, discomfort and disconnectedness and wonder why.

My body was tied up in knots by the time I got off the plane. Lucy stood in the lobby of the airport looking beautiful as ever and as distant as Mars. We held each other, and I could feel her tight shoulders even if I couldn't feel my own.

"Good morning," she said.

"Good morning." I knew something was wrong. We drove to a restaurant downtown, speaking only superficially. I ordered my eggs and toast and she looked at me, took a deep breath then turned away.

"What is it, Lucy?" I asked, not really wanting to know the answer. She turned and faced me, paused and looked away again.

"John, I can't do it. I just can't do it."

My soul rushed out of my body. My throat became dry. My stomach tightened up into one big knot.

"What do you mean, you can't do it?" I knew exactly what she meant but needed to pretend for another few moments and keep the pain at bay as long as possible.

"I mean I can't commit. I can't move in with you. I just can't do it."

"Why? Goddamn it, Lucy! It wasn't more than 24 hours ago I was having all these doubts and you sounded as sure about all this as you could be. You made me promise not to come to any decision about all this until I got here and in less that 24 hours you've made your decision without even talking to me. Damn you. I trusted you. I believed you. You're just running away from me and yourself and the relationship." I went on like this for 15 minutes or so until I finally said, "Tell me the real reason you can't do this, goddamn it."

Lucy got quiet, looked out of the window again and turned and faced me. "Because I think I love Robert. I know I have to try to be with him. I know I can't, but I just can't tell him goodbye. I can't stop seeing him just yet. I've tried."

I was so hurt I couldn't get angry just then. She had never said goodbye to Robert and never really told him about me. Deep down inside I'd known this all along but pretended that I didn't. I wanted to believe that everything was okay and that she could be who I wanted her to be, that I could believe her words and ignore her actions. During the previous six or seven months I would avoid asking about her relationship to him as much as I could.

When I did, she'd say, "We're just friends." And I'd try to believe it because I needed to. But all the time, all I did was deny my reality once again.

Most of us ACoAs grew up denying our reality. "Mamma, what's wrong with Daddy? He's acting funny." "Nothing, honey. He's just sick. Go on to your room. It'll be all right." We knew something was wrong.

"Mamma. What's wrong? Is something the matter?" As she tried to hide the tears, "Nothing, darling . . . Mamma's just tired. Everything will be okay . . . Don't you worry."

I worried. Something was wrong and every bone, muscle and organ told me so. And when they'd tell me, "Nothing," I began questioning my understanding of truth and reality, not to mention my intuition. Those formative years taxed my God-given ability to sense danger and dysfunction.

Sometimes parents just get plain ridiculous when they deny our reality as children and later as adults. Remember as a kid when you'd take those long trips in the car with your parents? When a two-hour drive to Grandma's seemed like forever? While counting cars, cows and barns, which was fun, you'd keep checking out the progress every few minutes, "Are we there yet? Are we there yet?" Most adult children are still asking that question of themselves and their therapist: "Are we there yet?"

Remember telling a parent ten minutes into the trip, "I have to go to the bathroom." And they'd somehow mysteriously know your reality far better than you, and you believed it when they said, "No, you don't . . . You just went to the bathroom before we left." Maybe you did, maybe you didn't have to back at the last gas station where Dad got another six pack and went to the bathroom. The message: Dad/Mom knows your bladder better than the body it's in — yours.

Or maybe you remember dinner time. Ah . . . dining with an alcoholic could be so enlightening. They'd put food on your plate . . . they knew what you should like and how much of it you should eat and what they'd do to you if you didn't.

"You will eat these brussel sprouts, young man, and you will like them."

One of my all-time favorites was that somehow they always knew when I should be sleepy. When things were crazy around the house, one of my mother's favorite phrases was, "It's time for you kids to get to bed." It didn't matter that it was four in the afternoon. A favorite father phrase was, "If you don't get to sleep, I'm coming in there and wear you out and you'd wish you were asleep." An all-time oldie but a goodie was sometimes when I'd be crying, usually after a whipping/beating by Dad, he'd demonstrate his superior intelligence with statements like, "If you don't stop crying, I'll give you something to cry about." And how many a mother has said, believing it to be so, "I know your own mind better than you."

So between our dad smelling awful and lying crumpled up on the stairs, mom shedding buckets of tears, them knowing our bladder, our bellies, our sleeping patterns, our pain threshold and our mind, I see why we were so afraid that if they ever left, we'd be in big trouble. And in the meantime I never learned to trust my own reality.

Set up to have to deny our reality as children, we continue to practice our parents' patterns right through most of our adult lives. Men deny the pain in their bodies. Hell, most deny they have bodies. Women still deny themselves for men in spite of the feminist movement. Men and women tell themselves a relationship is working or will work someday, when it hasn't worked since the third month of their meeting and will probably never work, no matter how many self-help books they use or counselors they visit.

When I was with Lucy, I was not getting the majority of my needs met most of the time. I was like the man or woman working at a job they can't stand but where the security and money are good. Most of us feel that some job is better than no job and that having some partner is better than being alone. We deny our reality. I denied mine and didn't even know it.

Many nights I'd lie in bed after Lucy had gone to sleep and wonder what I was still doing in this relationship. I'd think to myself that she/we had so much P.O.T.E.N.T.I.A.L. . . . If I could be loving enough, good enough, funny enough, love her pain away enough, maybe she'd love me. I tried, and in the process I totally lost touch with who I was and what I needed. I was in denial. It wasn't working. It hadn't worked, and until I changed some old patterns, it wouldn't.

After hearing the message, "abandoned again," loud and clear, Lucy and I drove to the house in silence. Then something began happening to my body, something I'd never before experienced to such an intense degree. The words she spoke at breakfast were penetrating my thin skin and going right to the core of me. I began shaking and trembling. I started sweating, my body began jerking slightly and I was running a slight fever. I was feeling nauseous and scared. I didn't know what was happening. It was as if the flu had descended on me in a matter of moments. Yet something told me it wasn't the flu.

Lucy and I went into a local grocery to buy some food for the evening, since I couldn't get a flight out until the next day at the earliest. I went into the store with her but had to leave because my legs felt as if water coursed through them instead of blood. My temperature was rising, so I left the building and went outside into the 90-degree weather, shivering.

Lucy came out and I told her how I was feeling. "John, what you describe sounds like the flu or some kind of withdrawal to me." Her words hit me hard. I was embarrassed and shaken by the possibility. I got in the car and we drove home. I got into bed and began convulsing and crying. Sweat was pouring off me. Lucy held me some and tried to console me.

"Goddamn it. I don't want you to see me this way," I began yelling. "I hurt so much and I'm scared and I don't know what's happening to me." Neither Lucy nor I really knew. We were both just letting the events and the feelings come. I kept convulsing and shaking and crying. After about 30 minutes I began to get some insight into what was going on by listening to what was coming out of my mouth.

"Mom, please don't leave me. Please. Please. Please don't leave me." I kept repeating this phrase, alternating it with, "Everyone has always left. I don't want to be alone. Dad, please don't leave. Please don't leave me."

The tears came. The rage. The feelings of abandonment at a physical level like I had never experienced before. At one point I turned to Lucy, who was observing it all, and screamed, "Go away. Get out of here. Leave me alone." She got up and left the room, thinking that's what I really wanted. "Please don't go. Please don't leave me alone." She came back and held me as I went through the physical, emotional process of experiencing and expressing the feelings of abandonment I experienced as a child with both my mother and father. After two-and-one-half hours of shaking, crying, kicking, screaming, I went to sleep. I slept very fitfully and finally awoke from an incredible dream at two a.m. This dream altered my life as much as the last two-and-one-half hours would. It would help to break a lifelong pattern and help me to overcome a life long fear . . . the fear of abandonment.

In the dream I walked slowly through several rooms of a house I knew all too well. As I went through each room, the things appeared out of corners, sides and ceilings. What came into view were symbols for a life split in half. Doors halfway open but not wide open. Windows half opened, half closed. Water in glasses that were only half full. Light streaming through to light up only half of the room. The images came in succession until I woke myself up with a scream.

"What is it, John? What's wrong?" Lucy was almost as shaken as I from having awakened so suddenly.

I was crying and freezing in a 90-degree Mississippi night. I got out of bed. Lucy got up and we went outside. I looked into the sky and started crying. "My whole life has been just half of what it should have been. I got half the love and attention I needed from my parents. My dad was there maybe half the time at best. My mom was a half-time mom at best. At worst they weren't there at all, but they never were fully there for me. They abandoned me a long time ago. When I was two or three instead of 35, I needed my dad and my mom to be there." I knew I was a child lying in bed that morning going through the most painful withdrawal of all. The withdrawal of love and affection and support that was never, ever there and if it was, it was unintentionally but undeniably half hearted.

I grew up thinking half was whole, and if you got half love, just half, then that was better than nothing. Being a child from a dysfunctional family, half seemed like all, since I never had any other standard to measure it against. Getting whipped, beaten, rejected, ridiculed, shamed, embarrassed, abandoned was what I, my cousins, my friends, my brother and sister saw and experienced. We all thought this was the way everybody in every family behaved.

I turned to Lucy, who stood against a street lamp. "Lucy, you were with me half the time, half there, half gone, half in love with me and half in love with Robert. And I thought it was enough, that that's all anyone ever gets, ever deserves. I believed that your wanting to make love one-fourth to one-half the time I did was enough. I needed to tell myself that wanting someone to be fully present, fully willing to love and be open was just too much to ask from anyone, especially since I'd never done it myself. But Lucy, something tells me, especially after that dream, that one-half just isn't enough. I deserve more in life. I'm not sure how to get it or give it. But half is not acceptable any longer." The tears subsided. A corner had been turned, but the pain was yet to be faced and felt.

I decided to stay until Sunday, the day I was scheduled to fly back to Austin. Saturday afternoon, Lucy and I went to dinner. The chills and the cramping had subsided temporarily. We dined mostly in silence and then went for a walk. My spirit hung heavy, my soul hid in the swamps and my discomfort increased as the moments we had together decreased.

"Lucy, I'm very sick. What we did, the way we did it, the things and feelings I denied tell me I'm much sicker than I thought."

Lucy was agitated by this. "John, you're not sick and neither am I. We just made a mistake."

"No, Lucy. There's something very wrong. I don't understand what it is. I don't know what to call the sickness but there is something disease-like about all of this, and I'm not sure about it but I know that I'm sick."

"No," she said firmly. "I'm not sick and neither are you, and we're not diseased either. We just moved too fast."

We talked on this way for a while. I knew that I, who had been lecturing and doing workshops on feelings and "flying boys," was very out of touch again with my own feelings. I was denying reality, minimizing my pain, putting her feelings first and still needing to be needed by her and others to feel good. Though I didn't know what to call this strange disease that came and went, I knew it hurt and minimized my chances for a healthy relationship. I knew I needed help.

That evening we decided to sleep together for what we thought would be the last night. About two a.m. I awoke from a fitful sleep and finally decided I was angry about all this. I had been angry before and had been teaching people for a couple of years how to get in touch with their anger and let it out appropriately. I turned towards Lucy. "Wake up, Lucy," I said in a quiet, gentle voice. She didn't hear me for two or three more tries. "Wake up." She finally rolled over and faced me.

"What?" she said in a half-asleep, half-awake voice.

"I'm angry," I said.

"What?" she said wearily.

"I'm angry," I said again in a low monotone.

"It doesn't sound like it. Wake me up when you really are, if you want to." She rolled back over and went back to sleep. I realized that, while I "knew" I should be angry, I still had trouble feeling the anger because I was afraid to show it with someone who meant so much.

There are many reasons people are afraid to feel their anger. As children, we learned at an early age this emotionally devastating equation: anger equals pain. Many of us decided that if we didn't feel anger, there wouldn't be pain. Children in dysfunctional families almost always witnessed anger expressed inappropriately when it was expressed. When someone in my family got angry, someone got hit, hurt, rejected or reprimanded, but never supported. In many families the feeling conveyed was, "Nice girls don't get angry" and, "Neither do good boys."

In my sessions for ACoAs and my men's groups it is obvious who the nice girls and good boys are. They usually smile and say they're not angry or smile even if they say they are.

Many people like myself saw anger — or I should say rage — inappropriately displayed and decided to do everything possible not to be like that painful parent. For instance, I saw Dad hit and Mom stuff. Between the two primary models I sometime, somehow unconsciously chose to be like my mom with regard to my own anger. Stuffing seemed nicer than hitting.

I've had clients who didn't ever see their parents get angry. They silently surmised that if anger was anything but evil, surely Mom and Dad would show it. Since they didn't, they assumed it best to do the same.

There seems to be one common denominator in all this. Every adult child is afraid if they really get angry and let the other person, whether partner, boss or parent, see it, that person might not like them and might leave them.

And since most of us have been left far too often, we'll do damn near anything we have to in order to insure that we won't be left again. So we stuff it, eat it or let it ooze out in passive/aggressive ways.

And most of those who do "let out their anger" would be surprised to find that, more often than not, they probably are not expressing it appropriately. That is another reason why many of us do not let our anger out. We don't know how to do it without blowing the other person out of the room. Very few of us really believe that anger is just a feeling, just a healthy emotion like sadness or joy. Most of us are scared of it and afraid of being left or hurt in some way if we show it.

Many women I have worked with over the last few years are so afraid of their anger that they put out this God-given fire with their tears. I, too, used to do this. Years ago, on the rare occasions I would let myself feel angry, I would start crying. It took me years to realize why I cried. I was sad that I didn't know how to be angry and let it out; I was sad because I couldn't let it out as a kid and still be loved and accepted. I came to understand that while sadness and anger usually go together hand in glove, tears are for sadness, not anger.

Most of us get angry sometime during our lifetime, sometimes a lot, but many men when asked, "Are you angry?" say "No." "Are you angry that your dad wasn't there for you?" "No, I understand he was just doing the best he could. He had it real rough growing up during the depression and all." When asked why they are afraid to let out their anger, the response that comes back from nearly all the hundreds of men and women I've worked with is almost word for word the same: "If I ever felt my anger, I'd tear this whole room apart and everything in it, including you, John."

This is parallel to asking them what they are afraid of about feeling their sadness. "I'm afraid that I'd start crying and never stop . . . that I'd drown me and you in my tears."

Consequently adult children are seldom comfortable and safe enough to really express years of pent-up, justifiable rage and anger. Thus they force themselves to appear as if everything is fine.

What most people don't realize is that anger is energy and energy begets energy. Energy held in and held on to tires and ultimately depresses us. Anger is a useful energy that helps us leave unhealthy situations, correct injustices, enhance communication and increase the possibility of intimacy. Anger held in and held onto will make us bitter, resentful and finally sick. But most of us are afraid that if we're angry and show it, we will pay dearly and probably be left. I've heard this from hundreds of my clients when asked, "How did you feel when such and such happened or was said?"

"I was angry."

"Did you tell them you were angry?"

"No."

"Why not?"

"I was afraid."

"Afraid of what?"

"Afraid they might leave."

"And if they left?"

"I don't want to be alone."

And if you read my first book, you know one of the reasons Laural left me was because I couldn't, wouldn't, was too scared to show my feelings . . . especially anger. Most of us have been left with our anger running through our veins, tissues, muscles and memory. Those that we were afraid would leave, did — either physically, spiritually or emotionally — and we ended up being alone, the very condition we went through every kind of contortion to avoid.

I was afraid to show my anger to Lucy that night because the little kid in me who was taught never to be angry at a loved one was afraid he would be left. And she had already told the man in me she was leaving. The anger finally came a few weeks later, and when it did, I felt much better.

Adult children from dysfunctional families usually have delayed responses to people, places and, most of all, their own feelings. Many of us have difficulty knowing what we think and feel, especially since we spend so much time and energy trying to figure out what the whole world is thinking and feeling.

My response time to situations charged with meaning and feeling was usually quite long. If I got angry at someone on a warm spring day in April of 1979, I probably wouldn't know it until the winter of 1985. Clients and friends say things like, "God, that really scared me or pissed me off." "When was that?" I'd ask. "Six months ago." But they were just now beginning to feel it.

The length of response time to our feelings about things is in direct proportion to our ability to de-armor ourselves and inhabit and feel our own bodies. Most adult children are so heavily armored due to destructive upbringing that it takes several failed relationships or major losses of any kind to begin stripping off the armor. Most of us tend to disassociate and leave our bodies when there is conflict, particularly if we or someone else is angry. We just fly away and don't feel the tightness in our shoulders or the tension in our lower backs and stomachs. So our response time is usually quite long.

As I got ready to leave Lucy and the memory of that weekend behind, we got closer as per usual. I was feeling better and was really trying to understand what she was going through.

"So I guess I won't be moving into our apartment. You can keep the stuff you brought from my house. How are you going to pay for this place by yourself?"

"I don't know. Something will work out. It always does somehow. I need to ask you something and I want you to know if you need to say no, I'll understand and I hate that I even have to ask."

For a man who needed to be needed as much as I did, I couldn't imagine saying "No," but I was damn sure going to give it a good shot no matter what the question.

"I don't have the money to pay next month's rent and it's almost due. I was wondering could you loan me the money. I promise I'll pay you back." She looked at me with those magical eyes. The word "no" kept repeating itself in my head over and over and over again.

"Yeah, I'll loan you the money. Don't worry about paying me back. You can pay me when you can."

Lucy drove me to the airport in silence. While she was tentative, she was also tender and touched by the pain she knew I was feeling. On the plane back to Austin I made a vow to myself, to God and to all women, children, men, dogs and cats that I was going to heal whatever disease of thought, body and spirit I was plagued with.

I went to the bookstore on Monday and the Adult Children of Alcoholics and Co-dependency sections drew me like a magnet. For the first time in my life I was ready to spend time in a section of the bookstore that I had successfully avoided my whole adult life. When I entered that large section and began thumbing through the books, I quickly knew why.

For years, in my quest for healing and happiness, I'd read everything from Billy Graham to Tibetan Buddhism, Freud to Norman Vincent Peale, but I wouldn't dare read Janet Woititz, Earnie Larson, Anne Wilson Schaef, Rokelle Lerner or anyone else writing about Adult Children of Alcoholics.

You see, I didn't know my dad was an alcoholic until my early 30s. I knew he drank a lot, but as a kid I accepted his definition of an alcoholic: "An alcoholic is a staggering drunk in a gutter who can't hold down a job." He always believed, and so did I, that since neither of us missed a day's work because of alcohol consumption, we weren't alcoholics. It was not until that very day that I became ready to know and admit I was an "Adult Child of an Alcoholic" and come out of denial about everything that admission would mean.

With denial left behind me, I looked more closely at my dad's drunkenness and my mom's co-dependency. True to my compulsive patterns, I dove into my pain by practically buying the store out and began reading nonstop. I began attending ACoA and Al-Anon meetings. For 28 days I put myself through a period I'll never forget.

Each morning I'd get up and go into my spare room and sit, feel and remember. The chills, fever and convulsions would come up as I'd talk to an empty chair that contained Dad, Mom, Lucy, Laural and others. The tears and the anger came up and were felt, experienced and released. The fear of abandonment was faced for the demon it can be and was slowly but surely exorcised from my being. It was like kicking alcohol or heroin. All the withdrawal symptoms were there, but unlike withdrawal from those drugs, I was able to control the process somewhat. I gave myself permission to feel and experience this pain but did not need to be hospitalized or secluded. Indeed, I found after 30 minutes or so of these sessions with myself, I could go on with the day's details. At night in bed alone I would go into cold sweats. My dreams were those of an addict looking for his stash, his connection, but in the form of people, particularly women. I was in a deeper stage of the same things I'd experienced after Laural left. Her departure had helped me heal and prepared me to heal some more old wounds common to all adult children.

During this time I began going to 12-Step meetings three to five times a week, sometimes two a day. At first I hated those meetings. I found reasons aplenty why they couldn't work and what I disliked about them. I needed to believe that my case was too unique and different and while this stuff might work for others, it wouldn't work for me. But I kept going and listening. I didn't talk for the longest time. I was afraid and angry and I wasn't sure I was safe with all these folks touched by the same disease as I.

Finally after about a dozen meetings or so some words came out.

"I'm John and I'm an adult child of an alcoholic."

"Hi, John." For months I hated it when they did that.

"And I'm angry that I have to be here and listen to all this shit but I needed to talk. Thanks."

I was angry for a while. I was finally understanding just how deeply my dad's alcoholism and his and my mother's need to put up with it had really affected my life and relationships all these years. It was like Dad and Mom should be at those meetings, not me. But I kept going anyway and hearing my story over and over again, from the debonair college fraternity boy to the overweight Mexican-American woman in the tight-fitting red chiffon dress. They were me and I them. We came from the same family. I realized why I hadn't wanted to ever go back to the first ACoA meeting a friend of mine had taken me to five years before. If I'd gone back, I'd have had to face things I didn't want to deal with.

I kept going and kept facing the pain, shaking, crying, journaling, screaming and praying like I'd never prayed before.

After a couple of weeks of meetings and many books read, I decided I was strong enough that I wanted to talk to Lucy and maybe see if we could be friends or somehow work this stuff out. Now I realize I was just needing a hit, another dose, a fix. I got it.

I flew in a week later with the words, "Yes, John, come on in, I'd like to see you." I flew in and before I got there she had flown away again.

Getting ready to go see Lucy again, after all I'd been through, was as pleasant as a walk over hot coals and as alluring as heroin to a confirmed, confined addict. I was scared and afraid the woman who wanted me over the phone would leave me alone again once I was there in person. But I also couldn't help but hope that maybe this time it would be different. She sounded so good. Maybe she had changed. Maybe she had left that other guy, come to her senses and realized that I was the best fish in the sea and wanted to reel me in.

With hope in heart, I boarded the plane. She picked me up at the airport. Again, I could see the same thing I'd seen before as soon as we'd get close. Right before my eyes, she became the incredible invisible woman. My heart sank into my stomach.

The feelings of abandonment came front and center.

We decided to check into a Holiday Inn. We were about an hour's drive from her home and both of us were tired. We talked and I could tell that nothing had really changed.

Earnie Larsen says it best: "If nothing changes . . . nothing changes." Most of us keep doing the same old thing and wonder why things don't change and we wonder why we do the same old things. One reason is that if we and those we interact with keep doing the same dance, we know how things are going to come out. While this hurts, it also gives us the illusion of control. Since most of us are control freaks to a greater or lesser degree, we'll do anything to feel that we have some control.

By doing the same things, we reduce the fear of the unknown, since we seldom enter into it any other way except by kicking and screaming. Sounds like childbirth, doesn't it?

As children we had almost no control over the chaos we were drowning in. I think some of us decided that if we ever got some control, we'd never give it up again to another person — not even to God. And then we wonder why God doesn't help us when we call.

Nothing had changed for Lucy and me. It was five a.m. as I lay in bed staring into space, right beside a naked woman who reminded me of someone in my past. I felt alone, abandoned and my needs were unmet again. Suddenly, strikingly, the pattern became clear. I was sad, excited and angry. I woke Lucy up.

"Tell me who this sounds like. 'Honey, if you'll just take me back, I promise I'll stop drinking. No, I mean it this time. I really will. Just give me one more chance. I'll make it up to you. Just let me come back.' " I paused and then went on. "Okay, but you really have to be different and the drinking has to stop. I'll try it one more time, but this is the last time. I mean it — it's the last time. If you don't stop, me and the kids are leaving." There was quiet and then a heavy sigh. "That's my dad and mom," I told her.

Lucy said, unable to hold back the tears, "It's my dad and mom, too."

Both my father and her father were alcoholics and our moms were co-alcoholics. As a child I grew up hearing the words I quoted to Lucy. My mom was forever taking him back and giving him second chances that turned into chance number 72, 73, 74, etc. I grew up listening to those talks, seeing those patterns, seeing boundaries not established or maintained and needs not met.

"Lucy, you are like your dad and my dad and I'm your mom and my mom. I hate it, and this may sound crazy, but even though you don't drink you're an alcoholic and I'm doing the same thing my mom did with my dad. You're a goddamn alcoholic just like our dads, and you keep asking for second chances and I keep giving them."

She and I were both crying. Pierced by the truth, confused by the rightness of the words, we lay there and held each other.

"You're right. I know you're right," she said again and again as we watched the sun come up.

It was only weeks later that I became familiar with the term "dry drunk." It describes people who have stopped drinking but continue thinking and behaving in the same old dysfunctional ways because they don't work a recovery program that is sufficient to change their personality. It also applies to people who do not drink alcoholically.

I didn't know until that night just how much Lucy and I had inherited many of the emotional and behavioral traits and habits of our alcoholic parents. We'd go on dry drunks ourselves without even knowing it. I realized that I had been a dry drunk for years. With certain people in certain situations, I'd act like a drunk, sometimes to the point that I'd black out, disassociate and distance myself from myself and my feelings and others. It was just what my dad would do when he was drinking.

That night I got in touch with just how much I was behaving like my mom in this relationship with Lucy. Mom had modeled this behavior for me growing up. Anger and sadness came up around this, and I knew I must not deny it. But I was sad because I finally had seen what had been going on as I'd never seen it before, and I saw just how deep my family's disease really was.

Once home, I made my way back into the self-help section and discovered *Co-dependent No More* by Melody Beattie. I read it and wept. There was a word for what I was feeling, being, denying and most of all a word that described my disease — co-dependency. Much later, I'd find that in my mind and heart the term co-dependent would describe my whole family's dysfunctional way of loving, interacting and hurting each other.

What is co-dependency and who is the co-dependent? I read a couple of books and still could not answer this question until after I had that last visit with Lucy. Upon returning home, I was feeling desperate and despondent with a disease I didn't really know I had. But I knew I had to do something.

I decided to call Wayne Kritsberg, a major figure in the ACoA movement. He had written several good books, and I had just recently read his *Adult Children of Alcoholics Syndrome*. I got an appointment with him a few days later. It was in his office that I finally understood what co-dependency is and that I am a co-dependent.

We began talking and I told him about the last few months with and without Lucy. Wayne is a graying wise fellow, almost always with a whimsical look in his eyes. He listened as we sat surrounded by pillows and plastic bats. I knew I was safe because his office looked so much like my own. Finally the words that I'll never forget came rolling out of my mouth and together with his own words — I got it.

"So, what do you need to do for yourself about all this?" he asked, looking into my eyes as if the answer would come from them.

"Well, what I need to do is not call her anymore. And what she needs to do is to call me."

Without even a pause, "How do you know what she needs?" he asked. I looked at him like he was crazy. I thought to myself, "This guy doesn't get it." I'm in the business to know what other people need. I've been with Lucy for almost a year. I secretly studied her every move, examined her thoughts, observed her mannerisms and body posture and was probably more in touch with her feelings than she was. And, after all, I grew up trying to figure out what Mom and Dad thought, felt and needed. I'd had a lot of practice. How else could a child survive if he didn't know what other people needed?

"Well, Wayne, I just know. I need to not call her, and based on her history and ways of doing things, she needs to call me."

"John, on our best day we may know some of what we need for ourselves, but only Lucy knows what she really needs."

At that moment it was as if I were dying. The lives of all the women I'd been with flashed before my eyes. My mom's and dad's lives flickered across my mental screen. I wanted to scream. "You mean I didn't know what all those people needed? I was wrong? Is that why all those women were so angry with me all the time?"

I had spent so much time trying to figure out what everybody else needed, that if I asked myself, "John, what do you need right now?" I wouldn't have known. I had grown up in a house and a culture that taught me you must always put yourself and your needs last. Others must come first in order that you would not be branded with a large S . . . Selfish.

I saw everyone in my family not saying what they really felt for fear of hurting another's feelings. I saw Mom take care of Dad's needs and omit her own. I saw Dad overwork himself for us, then resent us in the process. I tried to survive my co-dependent home where each one of us learned to depend on what others thought or felt and to depend on work, alcohol, TV, Valium, religion, caffeine, nicotine, sugar and other things to make us feel good when we really felt abandoned. Take those things away and we were lost because the hole in our hearts had to be filled with something or someone. No one taught us to fill it with ourselves.

I was trying one more time to fill my hole with a woman. Finally I knew the name of the disease I had had since early childhood. I knew why I felt sick when Lucy left me emotionally or physically. I knew why I felt like dying when Laural said she was leaving. I knew why I'd go into withdrawal when you took alcohol, TV, sugar, work, sex and caffeine away from me. I knew that session put me into not only a deeper understanding, but deeper into recovery, though not totally out of the relationship with Lucy.

Right after that session, I went to my first Co-dependents Anonymous (CoDA) meeting. This powerful 12-Step program is an offshoot of AA. The first one I went to included 12 women and one other man. While it was similar in style and form to the Al-Anon and ACA meetings I had been attending, it was different in subtle and overt ways. The focus was almost totally on ourselves and our feelings, rather than our parents or our childhood. While Mom and Dad or partners were discussed, it was substantially different.

When each person talked, it became obvious that in these meetings there would be no cross-talk between members of the group. Many times in my ACA and Al-Anon meetings, someone would raise their hand, not to tell the group what was going on with them, but to be recognized by the chair so they could address what the last person said and try to "fix" them by making comments or suggestions for things they "ought" to consider doing. It always made me nervous when this happened, and sometimes I'd feel very angry and excluded.

It took several CoDA meetings before I figured out why. As long as each person talked about where they were and what was going on with them, they usually held everyone's undivided attention. But when someone started talking to just one other person in the group, it felt like an old dysfunctional family pattern. It was like being at the dinner table where Dad would talk to Mom but not us, or my sister would talk to my brother but not the rest of the family. I'd watch the group. Eyes would wander, people would cough and fidget until the person stopped cross-talking and fixing and began to address the group as a whole unit.

Something was very different about me, though, due to all the work I had been doing on myself before my confrontation with the term co-dependent. In many ways I had learned some things about taking care of myself.

When Lucy and I broke up, I asked myself one very important question: "What is the best possible thing I can do for myself to get through this as quickly as possible and in a healthy way?"

When Laural left a few years before, the first thing I did to deal with my pain was turn to the patterns my parents taught me. I drank, I ate sweets and junk food, and I didn't exercise. I got sick and exhausted before I finally turned to a Higher Power, healthy food, therapy and exercise. This time would be different. I joined the YMCA so I could work out regularly. I hired a cook to make this noncooking bachelor healthy meals. I went to 12-Step meetings, got a sponsor, stayed in touch with friends and sought out a good therapist who specialized in ACAs and co-dependency. I got therapeutic massages on a regular basis and took some time off from work. I released tons of tears and I appropriately expressed the anger I was feeling towards Lucy and my father and mother by pounding a punching bag almost daily.

While there were many patterns from the past still planted in my consciousness, the more destructive ones had been rooted out for the weeds they are. No alcohol, no sugar, no caffeine and very little TV all equalled a lot of feelings, a bunch of memories and quite a bit of discharge. Within a couple of months the pain was beginning to fade, my inner child began to emerge and the belief that I had changed was beginning to feel true.

A very interesting thing was happening to me during this time. Right after Lucy told me she wasn't going to be able to live with me. I went into those withdrawal-like symptoms and the childhood fear of abandonment came up like never before. With all the shaking, crying, screaming and swearing that came out, some other habits began dropping off without my awareness. During those 28 to 30 days when I put myself through my own detox and detach program, I stopped wanting coffee, alcohol (my main drug of choice) was out; I could hardly stand to watch television and sugar sickened me.

Now all these things were the great comforters and numbing agents that I had grown up depending on. For years if I woke up feeling low or lonely, a couple of good strong cups of coffee and a cheese Danish would knock back down any feelings trying to surface. The caffeine would give me a zing along with the temporary rush from the sugar, and I'd be so far from feeling that I could go on, although I was almost always depressed. At night when I'd come home to an empty house, a couple of hours of TV and I'd sign off any memories or thoughts I might tune in if I turned off the tube.

In my family, as in most, when things were the worst, sugar was a source of comfort. "Run along and get yourself a candy bar. Momma's all right . . . nothing's wrong." "Go in your room and watch TV, everything is all right."

In the evenings we ate quickly, often in front of the TV with Dad watching the screen and his newspaper, too tired to talk. He was so hooked on sugar himself that he'd go for a drink so he could swallow a (sweet) sense of false security.

We were all junkies looking for a fix and finding one available almost everywhere we went. A TV in every home, a candy machine on every corner, in every restaurant a strong cup of Joe. Throw in cigarettes at 13 for me, alcohol, a good dose of sex now and then, and the painful trauma of my childhood and all the feelings I'd stuffed could stay away almost indefinitely. It took me years to understand most forms of depression are due to the inability to feel one's feelings. Depression is not a feeling. It's a lack of feeling or inability to feel. Many people confuse sadness and depression. Sadness is a feeling that if felt, passes like anger or frustration. Sadness, like anger, has been so misunderstood and thus so avoided that most people feel depressed a good portion of their lives. Sugar, caffeine, nicotine, alcohol, work, sex, TV, if used in inappropriate doses, all will numb out the feelings we have. Depression will result. The deeper we can go into and experience our sadness, the deeper we can experience our joy. If we run from our feelings of sadness and anger, we avoid joy and happiness as well.

During that time of intense work and release and dealing straight ahead with my fear of abandonment, those things I call secondary addictions began dropping off on their own. The purpose that they had always served was no longer necessary. They came to be seen as the true impediments to health that they really are if used in a dysfunctional way. As they dropped off, my feelings came to the surface more quickly and were experienced and expressed more readily. Health and healing were closer than ever before.

During a talk with a good friend and psychologist, Dr. Larry Benoit, I realized that as a very young child I turned to or was given sugar to comfort and nurture me at times when my parents could not. Later in adolescence and adulthood, sugar became one of my main sources of emotional sustenance. So the substance that comforted in childhood became an adult addiction. If I was beginning to feel sad or lonely or scared, sugar helped me survive. But during the talk with Larry, I realized that sugar takes me out of the world of feeling and into the world of depression — and thus away from my essential self — in a round-about, very indirect, seemingly harmless and legal way. I abandoned myself very much like I was abandoned as a child. The very things I used, whether sugar, caffeine or sex to try to numb out the pain and comfort the captive child trapped inside me, became that which perpetuated the feeling of abandonment.

I realized that the real addiction, the thing I was hooked on the most, was not sex or sugar or alcohol, but the abandonment. That is what I knew as a child, that is what became the normal condition. I learned to misuse the different things available in my world to further a process I hated my parents the most for — abandoning me. In other words, the things I did to not feel abandoned were exactly the things that left me feeling depressed and, most importantly, abandoned.

From this I began thinking and seeing that most of the learned behavior I demonstrated only appeared to be trying to get me the love, nurturing and intimacy I wanted. In reality it was the very behavior that kept those things from occurring. For example, I thought and learned that if you really wanted someone, you went after them full force. Yet, if that person, like most of us, feared abandonment, then the sheer force of my will and efforts scared them and they'd run further away.

When Lucy seemed to me to be the furthest away, I would get scared that I was being abandoned. I would try to all but force her to be with me. This attempt to get fixed would do just the opposite. She'd go further away, leaving me feeling depressed and more abandoned. It was as if being abandoned or feeling abandoned was the norm and feeling close to someone was the oddity. I knew how to be alone, but not how to be with someone, and yet I knew I didn't want to be alone. Nearly everything I did, though, with every partner I picked, provided me with the feeling that I would be or was being abandoned.

Something I decided after reading Dr. Charles Whitfield's invaluable work, *Healing the Child Within*, is that adults cannot be abandoned. Adults cannot be abandoned. Yes, I know when you read that you probably thought, "This guy's crazy. I've been abandoned by some man or woman a dozen times since my 20s." That's the way I felt, too, until I realized that adults can't be abandoned. They can be left and they then can *feel* abandoned but they can't really be abandoned.

Imagine yourself as a child . . . helpless, dependent, needy. You depend on a parent for all your support and all your needs to be met. If they don't come, then you can't do a thing about it except hurt, maybe even die. This is perhaps the greatest fear in humankind, and feeling abandoned feels like we're going to die. You know those songs that say, "I can't live without him," "She's my reason for living." But adults can live without someone. Adults can support themselves and get what they need once they learn how.

Most of us haven't learned how to ask for what we need, so when our lover or parent leaves us, we feel defeated, defenseless and damaged. The child within feels left again, feels there's nobody home to take care of it. This feeling is even stronger because, usually, the moment we experience loss we turn to our drugs of comfort and further abandon our child within. We feel lost and numb until we find another mummy or daddy, or perhaps a partner who plays both parental roles too well. I realize now that Laural, my last love, and then Lucy, both could be just like my father and mother, depending on situations and circumstances.

The only way I can be abandoned is if I leave my Self . . . my inner child. I realize now why I was able to deal more effectively with the loss of Lucy than the loss of Laural. I had made some tentative contact with my inner child, instead of numbing my little boy with caffeine, alcohol and sugar the way I did when Laural left. Yes, I was sad, angry and hurt, but I was all right and not abandoned. I learned to stay with the hurt child inside. I listened to and nurtured that hurt little boy that time had all but forgotten.

Several patterns lingered for a long time. Every time I would begin to get strong, clear and centered, it seemed that Lucy would call or write — or I would call her. Most of those times she seemed to me to be down, depressed and a bit needy. We'd talk or see each other. After every one of those encounters, it felt as if my power flew right out of the window and I was left feeling lonely and angry. They seemed to leave Lucy feeling better and stronger. Then she wouldn't need me. I needed to be needed in order to feel good about myself. This kind of dysfunctional interaction was not unique to Lucy and me. I had felt it before with other people, particularly women, particularly my mom.

I learned at an early age that if I felt needed, I also felt loved. Therefore, when I wasn't needed, I didn't feel that anybody loved me. My mom needed me a lot, since she had chosen to be with a man who couldn't meet most of her needs. It was the natural choice for her, after having grown up in an alcoholic family system herself. I tried to meet my mom's needs. She let me, and we called it love.

One evening, long after Laural and I had broken up, I saw her leaving a theater we both were at. I stopped her and asked her to talk. We went to a nearby cafe. The lights were as dim as my spirit back then. I had promised myself that the next time I saw her, I was going to tell her something I'd never told anyone before. I thought that what I would say might get her back. I had tried everything. She was receptive, though a bit tentative. I held her hand. I looked her in the eyes, flew out of my body and heart and up into my head and said the words, "Laural, I need you. I really do need you." I had never said those words to anyone before, so I thought they were special and would win her heart over.

I had not used those words because after viewing and experiencing my mother's neediness and my parents' inability to meet my needs, I vowed somewhere in childhood that I'd never need anybody ever again, never admit I was lonely or needed anybody. Looking back, I can see I was very needy. Even my acting so self-contained was needy, rather than an attempt to fulfill a genuine need. Laural looked into my eyes and asked a question straight from her heart as her whole body became a prayer that I'd finally have the right answer.

"What do you mean, you need me?" It seemed there was only one right answer and if I could find it in that crucial moment, the woman I loved would return once and for all and we'd live happily ever after.

There was a long silence. I flipped through the dictionary in my brain looking for the right words. They weren't there. I, a walking, talking Hallmark card, who could always find the right words to suit every occasion, could only say, "You know I need you. I need you to be with me. Will you come back and marry me? I need you. I've never said those words before, Laural. I really need you." She knew it was still neediness, fear and co-dependency. It was not a genuine desire to be with her and share life as two whole human beings, each equally capable of giving and receiving.

Her countenance dropped, the light was extinguished from her eyes. The words weren't right because the feeling wasn't right. I still needed her to fix me because I still felt broken and didn't know how to take care of myself and hoped she would do that for me. I came from my head and not my heart for what must have been the thousandth time. I needed her because I still didn't have me.

It felt as if Lucy needed me sometimes the same way I needed Laural. I needed her and Lucy because there wasn't enough of me for me. One thing I know now is why when I was down and depressed, I was also dis-eased with co-dependency. I find for me one thing co-dependency is about is the unfair, unconscious exchange of energy.

When I was feeling low, lonely, lost and without energy, I'd call Laural, or intuition or reason would lead me to where she'd be. We'd talk, she'd hold me, I'd touch her hand and I'd be all right. She would leave feeling tired, disappointed at best, almost destroyed at worst, but I'd feel much better. Sometimes Lucy would call me feeling the same way. Before the call, I'd feel strong and clear. By the end of the call, I'd feel co-dependent and chaotic. She'd feel better. Sometimes the reverse would occur. I'd feel like shit and call — and presto-chango, I'd feel much better. It took being with another woman to realize some of what Laural felt and to get in touch with a phenomenon that had occurred all my life.

Babies are dependent and connected to Mom and Dad. When the umbilical cord is cut and the infant breathes in its first breath, the baby's heart, lungs and solar plexus become the space that is to be filled with the special energy only Love can provide. We suffered if we were born to parents whose own parents did not instill the life force in them. They needed us to feel their own empty hearts. By early childhood, our energy had been drained and drawn out of us, just as if our needy co-dependent incomplete parents had put straws in us and sucked out our essential selves.

Instead of constantly putting their love and energy into our hearts, they took it out — not intentionally and not maliciously, but because they had no other source. They consistently left us feeling depleted and tired, with little or no energy for our own lives. By early childhood I began giving unspoken permission to my mother to take whatever energy I had whenever she needed it. Unbeknownst to her she readily drank in this energy. She then felt better about her life.

If this sounds too strange, think about it a moment. Have any of you women ever felt strong, wonderful, clear — and then given up your power and energy to the first beautiful man you saw chock-full of potential? But then when you got with him and gave him your energy, he ended up feeling and looking even better and you ended up feeling depleted and defeated. Have you ever been around someone, then felt whipped out afterwards? When we give our energy, let our energy be taken this way, it is co-dependency in action. It is co-dependent in that we become a false self to satisfy another's insufficiency. Then we feel victimized, resentful, martyred and angry.

That energy we should have received and kept for ourselves as children was used instead to become what and who our parents needed us to be so they could feel better about themselves. The energy that was to be received and stored in our heart and abdomen was not there. Its absence hurt so much that we divided ourselves from ourselves. We left our heart center — our receptor for parental love and the love of our Higher Power. Instead we went up into our heads or down into our genitals or both to try to find the love we needed to survive.

As a kid, I quickly figured out what I needed to do, and who I needed to become, in order to be loved by the ones I needed the most. It was with my head that I turned off the painful void in my heart. It was with my brain that I escaped the reality of not getting what I needed. I flew up into my head and learned how to survive the painful emptiness of childhood.

In adolescence I lowered some of my energy into my genitals. I began thinking with my penis, hoping it would connect me back to somebody who would energize a life that was perpetually exhausted by the time I was 13.

I remember even as a teenager hunting for the perfect girl who would fill my empty heart. Never once had I been shown how to fill that hole with myself, so I sought and sorted through different women in hopes that one day I'd be complete.

Co-dependency is about many things. One of them is one person looking to another person, a substance or a process to temporarily provide them with the energy they need. This energy was taken from them as children or given to them inadequately. They are constantly seeking spiritual and emotional sustenance themselves. Co-dependency is also about using people, processes or substances to make us momentarily forget and not feel the hole that's in each of our hearts.

After I had spent several weeks soaking up all I could find on co-dependency and adult children issues, Lucy called, saying she wanted to be just friends. I made flight reservations, thinking I was strong enough to withstand any and all disappointments waiting on me as I learned to detach. But I also had a hope buried underneath all the pain. If Lucy could see just how co-dependent she was (or I thought she was), and if she'd make a concerted effort and commitment to work on it, we still might have something. The would-be Baptist preacher I never became was going to take the gospel of *Co-dependent No More* by Melody Beattie and beat her over the head with it if necessary to get her to see the error of her ways. Obviously I had not really mastered the first step of Co-dependents Anonymous, *"We admit we are powerless over others and that our lives have become unmanageable."*

We went to dinner that evening and had a tense but pleasant conversation until there was an opening and I told her about the term co-dependent. I thought she'd be receptive, since she had been attending Al-Anon and ACA meetings for a long time. The term itself is a slippery one for even those of us who really think we understand it. For those of us who are not ready, calculus is much easier to grasp and far less threatening.

When I began explaining to Lucy what I thought co-dependency was and how it worked, she became tense. I thought she would readily recognize herself as being co-dependent, since she, too, was an adult child of an alcoholic. It didn't go over so well. By attempting to take somebody else's inventory, I dropped deep into the disease, and she got very angry and frustrated. After about an hour, I was so co-dependent, I was a mess. I think she was, too.

Here's what it looked like and sounded like to me: She began pacing back and forth like a caged animal. I began getting terrified — my stomach knotted up and my shoulders went up to my ears. "Look, Lucy, if you can only understand what I'm trying to tell you, I believe we can get out of this disease together. All you have to do is take my hand, and we'll figure out a way to stop this shit, stop hurting and be together."

"Look, John, I can see you've got a problem. But I don't understand all this stuff about co-dependency. We just can't be together as lovers anymore, and you can't accept that and I can. I don't have a problem with this. I don't want to talk about this anymore. It's just another label and I'm tired of labels."

"Lucy, this relationship and this disease is both our problem, and if we don't both work on it, we can't be together."

"You don't get it. I'm fine. I don't want to be with you anymore in the same way you do and I don't even understand what you're talking about and I'm tired and drained and I refuse to discuss it anymore."

As she started walking out of the room, I yelled, "You're being co-dependent right now. You need me to not talk about this so you'll feel okay, because if I don't stop talking about it, you won't be okay."

God, did she get mad and mean after that . . . God, was I co-dependent or what?

I left the next day and flew to Santa Fe to give my first national workshop on *The Flying Boy/Wounded Man*. When I got there, I received a telephone call from Mary J., who is now a trusted and true friend. She called to tell me that she believed *The Flying Boy: Healing the Wounded Man* was one of the better books on co-dependency. She was recommending it to her clients and friends. While the book never used the word co-dependent, I too had just recently realized that Laural and I in that book were immersed in co-dependency. Neither of us knew the term at the time, but it now had a name. Finally I came to see that all the relationships I'd had since childhood were more addictive than loving, more co-dependent than caring.

I thanked Mary for the confirmation and for the support of my work. Then I went deeper into my own recovery process by going right into the belly of the beast . . . I went home to visit my family.

Before going home I had an idea based on the readings I'd done and the feelings that came up. I contacted my sister and asked her if once we all convened at her place, she'd be willing to go into family therapy. Kathy, who had been in therapy for a while, was open to the idea. I took it one step further, then, and told her about my idea to do an intervention with our dad. His alcoholism was becoming more pronounced. I was very worried about him, as well as feeling overwhelmed by how much that disease had figured in my own co-dependency. My sister was reluctant, but willing to cooperate. I then went one step further and asked her to be the coordinator and even the initiator of the whole thing. For 30-some odd years that role had been left to me to play, and I was rapidly approaching the age of retirement from being the Hero Child. Again she agreed, saying she'd set it all up. I then called my mom, who had never been in therapy or to a 12-Step meeting at this time.

"Mom, would you consider doing some family counseling while we're all in Nashville?" I asked. I didn't really know how she'd take this, but guessed that after having read my book, she'd be open to the idea.

."Yes, I would, but I don't think your father will want to do this."

"I want us to heal this disease that affects the whole family, and since it is still tearing us apart, I want to give it a try. Will you call Randy (my brother) and ask him to do this with us? Kathy is going to set it all up." I was hoping and praying that this effort to heal us would demonstrate the love we felt for Dad, each other and ourselves. But I also knew that most interventions do not succeed in the short run, though they may have multiple long-term effects on each person who participates and even those who don't. I knew my dad, who thought only "sick" or "crazy" people went to see therapists, would probably not see himself as one needing any outside help. But I knew I needed help. Perhaps it was worth the risk of angering him and alienating him from the rest of the family.

Flying to Nashville, I felt much as I did when I went home a year before, after not having seen my dad for four years. I was scared but hopeful. Dad and I had been having some great conversations over the phone ever since my book came out. He'd call me periodically, or I'd call him, and we'd talk openly and honestly. I began thinking, "I can go home and this man will really be there for me. At last, I'll have a dad . . . a father. And I'll forgive him, and he'll forgive me, and we can be close, even closer now that we can talk to each other. Maybe we could even be buddies, especially if he could stop drinking and get some help."

The plane touched down and my spirits rose. Scared as I was, I had faith it would all work out. My dad had called ahead and said he'd meet me at the airport. My hands were cold and clammy, my heart raced ahead of me ready to meet my dad, my eyes searched the crowd for his, and there he stood. But as soon as I saw him, I could see he was gone. The man who had been present over the phone had disappeared on me in person. I came up to him, hugged him, smelled the odor I'd come to hate and saw the phantom of a father I always saw as a kid. As we walked away he said, "I'd barely got here in time to get me a drink before you got here."

My heart sank as I realized this was the way it had always been. He just wasn't there, and he couldn't be. He'd hidden himself for so long. I knew that, try as we might, the intervention had to be something for me. I began accepting that I didn't cause my dad's disease and I couldn't cure it.

We drove to my sister's in silence, speaking only now and then on superficial subjects. I began to get really scared. I thought about turning around, getting back on the plane and flying away.

We finally arrived at my sister's house. Everyone was there except my brother, the "Lost Child." Within five minutes every pattern was in place. The tension increased proportionately with the alcohol in my father's blood. We talked at each other and not to each other. My sister, the peacemaker who always tried hard to get Dad to see my side and me to see Dad's, started her job. Mom, the martyr, said little, but on occasion sided with me. It was terrible. There were three days left of the visit, and we hadn't even faced the hardest moment yet. This was coming when Kathy would break her pattern and ask Dad to go to therapy with us. Meanwhile I knew I had to do something about all the tension I felt in my body. After about two hours of walking on eggshells, I decided to go for a run.

"Where are you going?" Dad asked, as I headed for the door in my running clothes. "I'm going for a run. I need to stretch out from the plane ride. I'll be back in a little bit."

"You just got here and you're already leaving?"

"Dad, I'll be back in a little bit." My voice went up an octave.

When I returned, I felt much better. The workout allowed me to concentrate on my breathing and my body, which reduced the fear and the tension. But as soon as I walked in, Dad walked out of the kitchen. I knew this meant he'd just had another shot. "Well, I'm glad you decided to come back. We've been waiting on you." His voice was tired, old and very tense. I felt shamed again and guilty that I couldn't tolerate as much insanity as my fellow family members.

Later in the afternoon, none of us had yet made contact with anything except the TV. It always seemed to be going when the family got together. I always said things like, "Can't we turn this thing off?" and Mom usually said something like, "I'd like it off, too," and Kathy would say "At least we can turn it down," turning toward Dad to see how he'd handle it. It would be obvious he wanted it on, so it got turned down a little. Each of us played our role from the scripts inscribed on our brains.

I began feeling crazy, scared and out of control. Yet I'd had enough time in the program to know I had choices and I could do something to take care of myself. Always before, I'd leave and not come back or stay and white-knuckle my way through. I'd wind up taking a few aspirins or antacids to help my body survive a family get-together. This time I decided to go to an Adult Children of Alcoholics meeting for a reality test and some support. I looked up the Al-Anon number in the Yellow Pages and found one close by. Dinner, which was terrible, clinched my decision. Dad almost always embarrassed me and, I think, the rest of the family whenever we'd eat out. That time was no different. He shouted commands at the waiters and waitresses in his attempts to exert control and live the illusion that money made him powerful. He felt that his paying for the meal bought him the right to shame and embarrass all who participated.

After dinner I told the family I'd be going to an ACA meeting and wouldn't be home until 10 p.m. or later. I gave myself plenty of time to tour Nashville afterward, in hopes they'd all be in bed when I returned.

"You're going to a what?" Dad asked, with a confused look on his face. He'd never heard the term ACA.

"Adult Children of Alcoholics meeting, Dad. It's part of AA. I've been going to them for a while back home and they really help me a lot."

"Why do you need help? What's wrong? There's nothing wrong with you."

Shades of childhood, when we'd travel and he'd tell me I didn't have to pee or I wasn't hungry. "Dad, I just need a meeting right now. I'll be home later."

As I started for the door, he yelled, "Damn if this ain't something — we drive all the way up here to be with you kids and you leave twice in one day. First, you go jogging and now to some damn meeting that I still don't understand why."

I walked out feeling crazier than ever. I was grateful for that meeting, for that island of sanity in what felt like an ocean of alcoholism.

I felt better, but my plan to avoid another encounter that evening failed. Dad was still up, still drinking and still Dad. When I walked in, the first words that came out were, "You're so selfish. You're the most selfish of all the children and you only think of yourself. Your mom has been wanting to see you and looking forward to this trip for a long time, and you leave her and your sister here and go off running and to some damn meeting for alcoholics. You're selfish, son."

Due to such little time in recovery, and so much time in a sick family, I was beginning to feel he was right. I had been taught by both the family and society that if you take care of yourself first instead of putting other's needs before your own, you're selfish. I began to think I was wrong for going to an ACA meeting and exercising. I thought, "Maybe he's right. I'm the sick one. Mom doesn't need a meeting. Kathy doesn't need to go for a run. Randy doesn't even need to be here, maybe he's the healthiest one of us all. And if I wasn't so damn selfish, I would have stayed." But thanks to my Higher Power and a lot of hard work those thoughts didn't last long. I knew what I did was right and healthy, and I was not going to let any "stinking thinking" win this time. I went to bed scared but okay.

The next morning during breakfast, my sister spoke the words that had more impact on our family than I ever imagined possible. "Dad" she said half heartedly, "we're going to therapy today and we want you to come with us."

Dad looked confused at first and then angry. "Well, I ain't going to pay any crook to hear my problems. I ain't got any problems. Psychiatrists are just a bunch of crooks who sponge off other people's misery. That's the way John makes his living, off other people. They're all a bunch of crooks and I don't need one. If y'all want to go see a therapist, go ahead but I won't go. We came here to visit you kids, and you let John talk you into going to therapy instead of us all going out and having a good time."

Dad barely paused. "Son, I know you have problems. You can't keep a woman, and I know you're upset about Lucy leaving you. If you need help, I just can't understand why. You're so smart. You've been to college and read all those books and you teach people and help them; I just don't see why you can't help yourself. You ought to be able to figure things out. I've never been to a therapist a day in my life, and me and your mother are happy. You could be, too, if you just put your mind to it. I ain't going, and that's all there is to it."

My hopes sank. I talked to Dad a bit after his monologue, but I don't remember what I said. Whatever it was it didn't change his mind. Shortly after lunch, Kathy asked Dad to drive us to our therapy appointment. Dad was nervous, but he acted calm and in control until my mom stepped out of the car to go with us into the therapist's office.

"Where are you going, Frances?" he said in a gruff but shaky voice.

"I'm going to therapy, Jimmy. Kathy told you we were going." Mom was terrified.

"You didn't tell me you were going. I thought just John and Kathy were going. You didn't tell me about this. Why didn't you tell me? You've known about this all along, haven't you? You've betrayed me. This is a trick. Well, I ain't going to fall for it. You get back in this car right now. You ain't going. Get in. We're leaving."

Mom's moment of truth came. Kathy and I looked at each other and then at her. Mom had always done what Dad said when it came to the big decisions of her life. That's the way she was raised, and that's what she thought a wife should do. I have never had much respect for Mom because of the way she let Dad dictate her life, never stood up to him and took the abuse he dished out. I held my breath. I thought for sure she'd give in once again to the alcohol, the disease and the dictate of country music and the Bible: "Stand By Your Man."

"Jimmy, I'm going to therapy with the kids. We want you to come, too. Honey, we love you and we need help, and I'm going to get help. I've never gone against you, but I'm going to therapy."

Mom's voice was as strong as I've ever heard. My mouth dropped open in disbelief. My sister was stunned. That was our mother. No it wasn't that was a Frances Lee we never knew existed. Somewhere in time she had changed.

"You get in this car right now. I'm leaving, and you're my wife, and you're going to do what I say. You're coming with me. I'm leaving. I'm going back to Florida right now, and you're going to go with me."

Mom turned and faced Dad. "Go on. Do what you have to do. I'm going to do what I have to do." We turned away from a floored father. He spun out of the parking lot and headed, we guessed, for the nearest bar. My mom headed into recovery and my sister and I headed into a brand-new relationship with our mom.

The therapy session wasn't easy and lots of tears came. We talked, and I told my mom and sister how I felt and they told me. We got closer than ever before during the first session. Because that session is ours and not mine, I need to respect my mom's and sister's privacy. What did come out, though, was an agreement to try again to get Dad to come back with us the next day. The therapist assigned us behavioral tasks for telling Dad that we were going back for another session. Performing those tasks almost killed me, as the process broke a pattern.

That afternoon when we got home, my sister's role, as explained by our therapist, was to be the talker. She was to make the request for Dad to come into therapy the next day. She would break her pattern of mediator. Mom was to support my sister in a direct way and give up her victim and martyr role. I was to be silent, sit still and stay in the room no matter what happened. I wasn't to do my usual pattern of trying to be hero, counselor, fixer or flyer.

The toughest part for me was to sit still. I realized that in early childhood, if something didn't go well or the chaos got too intense, I flew out the door like a jet. Only moments into our confrontation with Dad, I'd see where I learned that behavior.

I sat there and didn't open my mouth. I wanted to leave the room a thousand times in the course of five minutes.

My sister spoke to Dad gently but firmly. "Dad, I love you and I want to get some help and see our family get along better . . ." She went on for a few minutes. Then Mom joined in. "Jim, we're not saying you need help, we're saying we all do. This is a chance to get it while we're all here . . ."

My dad got scared. This moment in my history was one of the most important in my life. My dad got angry at me first, though I wasn't saying anything. "This is all your fault. You're to blame for this. You've always had problems and you want to blame me for them. You can't keep a woman and you think it's my fault. None of this would be happening if you hadn't made it happen. Well, there's nothing wrong with me . . ." He yelled and talked like this for over an hour, pausing only to go into the kitchen for shots of courage.

Turning on Kathy like a lion about to slaughter a lamb, he roared: "You, I've always trusted and loved. How dare you tell me I need help. You've been married three times, smoke pot, taken drugs and I never stopped loving you . . . I never told you if you didn't go into therapy I'd stop loving you."

This hurt me more than his barrage of attacks on me. I was used to that. But I knew Kathy really worshipped my dad and had always been there for him. Looking back, I can see how she parented him even as a little girl, much like I parented Mom. But at this moment fear consumed my dad, and he started biting his support the way a trapped animal chews off its own leg. Dad started yelling at Mom, Mom yelled at Dad, and I was five all over again. I was scared, anxious, sad, hurt. I wanted to jump out of my skin, out of the room and into my car and get the hell out of there because someone was about to get hurt. This madness went on for about two hours before it peaked. Finally in the eye of the hurricane that we called "our family," something happened.

My dad was yelling and screaming, heading for the door to leave permanently and about to carry out my worst childhood fear. It was a scene that would be forever imprinted on my mind. He stood with one foot in the house and one foot on the porch. He turned towards the three of us. There was a look on his face I'll never forget, and a recognition of many patterns all at once as he spoke. "You're leaving me. You've never loved me and now you're leaving me. You're driving me out because you don't love me and you never have. You all are leaving me." Dad had his suitcase in his hand and was standing there halfway in, halfway out.

I realized that person, that picture was Lucy with me. And it was me with Laural and others. I was always leaving. What passes for love to an adult child of a dysfunctional family is staying dysfunctional, not rocking the boat, keeping the secrets, holding in feelings and never getting help or changing. When Laural wanted me to go into therapy with her, I thought she didn't love me the way I was and if I didn't change, she'd leave. I didn't know she wanted us to get help because she loved me.

"Dad, we love you," I started screaming, "that's why we're doing this. You've always left me just like you're doing right now. We're here. You're the one who's got the suitcase. You're standing in the door telling us we're leaving you. I need you. I've always needed you, and you're leaving. You've always left. Please stay this time. Please stay."

Tears ran into my mouth as I moved toward him. My sister was crying, and so was Mom. Dad turned and came at me as if he was going to hit me. I picked up a chair to defend myself. One thing I knew was that he'd never hit me, Mom or Kathy again, no matter how much I loved him.

"Don't you yell at me. I'm your father. You have to respect me." At that moment I let go of both the chair and something I'd held onto my whole life — my father. The man coming at me was so scared, that I saw the face of a little boy. He was just a frightened little boy who wasn't capable of being anybody's father. This boy would never, ever be the father I needed as a child. He would never be the father I still longed for as a 35-year-old man.

At that moment I realized my dad had a disease and that his own inner child was in terror. I knew I had to let go of the wish, the hope, the dream that this man could someday be the father I had always waited for him to become. He couldn't in 1951, and he couldn't now that I was a man. I knew I had to let him go if I were to ever become the father my inner child desperately needed. I had to stop waiting and giving him opportunity after opportunity to become the man I wanted to be. I had to let go of this scared boy/man who hid himself in alcohol.

I dropped the chair. My dad cried, and I let go. He came back inside for a while and finally left.

I haven't seen him since, haven't needed to. I miss him sometimes, but I don't miss the toxic chaos. I still pray for his recovery, all the while learning to love him un-conditionally, even knowing I don't want to be around him for a while.

Tim came in the other day for a session. In his middle 30s, graying, good-looking, gaining a little extra weight around the middle, he still looks more like a boy than a man. Tim has gone back to college for the third time to try to complete his bachelor's degree. He's been married twice. Climbed up the ladder of success and fallen back down about three times. His father, like mine, is an alcoholic and his mother is dead.

Usually Tim wanted to work on his relationship to his parents as well as his own life. But today he wanted to talk about his dad.

He had called the week before to ask his dad if he'd help him and his newest girl friend buy a house so they could stop paying rent. Tim and the woman he was living with were not getting along very well since the third month of their whirlwind romance.

"My dad said he'd loan me the down payment, but he wants to come down from Houston to look at different parts of the city before he decides to give me the money," Tim began.

"In other words, he wants to be in on which house you buy?" I asked.

"Yeah, I told him that wasn't necessary, that I just wanted the money and that I'd pick the house and section of town I wanted." Tim sounded a little frustrated. "Then Dad said that he had been around and had bought a few houses in his time and knew what he was doing."

"So it sounds like he doesn't trust your judgment?" I asked.

"Goddamn right, he doesn't. He never has. He didn't like my first wife and told me if I married her, he'd disown me. And he thought my wanting to be an artist was silly. He wouldn't pay the bills and wouldn't pay for art courses at college, so the first two times I was in school I studied accounting. My dad's an accountant. I hated it, and I flunked out twice. He doesn't know that I'm taking art courses this time because I didn't tell him. After all, it's my education."

He paused and I made a guess. "Is he paying for your school stuff now?"

"Well yeah, I mean he's loaned me the money. But I'm going to pay him back. Anyway, I don't see what all this has got to do with me buying a house."

Tim at 33 was still giving his dad every possible opportunity to be the dad he never had been. But more importantly, he kept perpetuating the parenting he'd grown accustomed to, indeed depended on and was addicted to. Dad did his usual dance and Tim followed the steps to an alcoholic waltz. Tim wanted his dad to trust his decisions about school, women and houses. But Tim kept putting himself in the familiar role of boy-child. Dad then did the best he could with the role he'd always played — the role of Father Knows Best.

Tim couldn't see that nothing had changed about his dad regarding money and alcoholism. The strings that were attached as a kid were still there. Tim was angry, as if his dad was doing something different from what he'd always done. Tim was staying the boy who let his father loan him money and thus felt he had a right to say how it would be spent. Interestingly Tim always stayed just this side of success, even though he was talented and intelligent almost to a genius degree. For if he succeeded, how would Dad get another chance to rescue the boy? Who would give Dad a chance to be the dad the son always had dreamed of and longed for? Tim couldn't let go of his father without the fear that he'd float off into space.

I left Nashville hurt but hopeful, stunned yet strong. I decided I would never put myself and my inner child through that kind of trauma again for anyone. I knew that I'd had enough angry alcoholic abuse to last a lifetime. I knew that I needed not to see my dad for a while, at least until such time as he was willing to begin his own recovery journey. If that time never came, I knew I had told him how much I loved him. I knew I had finally started moving toward a true state of forgiveness. I knew that I had experienced and expressed the anger, hurt, rejection and sadness, as well as the love I felt for a man doing the best he could at the time.

Forgiveness. It's a blessed idea whose time refuses to come to some. However, many men and women I've worked with over the years have tried to get to forgiveness before they get to their feelings. Forgiveness as a concept not backed up by feelings is empty and meaningless.

"Ron, have you forgiven your mother for abandoning you?" I asked during a session.

"Sure . . . hundreds of times," was the answer.

There is a tendency in 12-Step programs, some orthodox churches and even some traditional therapies to get someone to forgive and forget before they remember and reclaim the lost feelings that must be experienced before true forgiveness can be theirs. I know I wanted to pray away the pain my dad dished out. Later I wanted to meditate the memory of my mom away. And later I wanted to bathe all my anger in the white light. I wanted to do anything but feel the hurt and loss. Many of my clients try to do the same, trying to follow a short cut to forgiveness.

Many feel that feeling the pain before the forgiveness is only "wallowing in self-pity," as some old timers will tell you at AA meetings. They often will shame a newcomer by yelling at him to "climb down off the pity-pot" and "put the past behind you." Many think that feelings before forgiveness is equal to blaming. However, it is quite the opposite.

Blaming and self-pity are demonstrated in a person's life when they refuse to own their repressed feelings about their family history. Self-pity is demeaning and destructive, but genuine grief and anger that come up when remembering are invigorating, energizing, dignified and cleansing.

Most of us blame ourselves for all that went wrong. I didn't cause my dad's alcoholism. It took me a long time before I discovered this. Somehow as a child I thought, with shame, that I was the cause. And if I were the cause, I had to find the cure or be the cure. If I were good enough, smart enough, athletic enough, cute enough, maybe Mom and Dad would stop arguing. Maybe Dad would stop drinking and be the dad I wanted so desperately. The fact is that as a child I had no choice but to be raised in an alcoholic/dysfunctional home. I do not believe children choose abuse, nor can they defend themselves.

There is not only grief and anger, but hope as well if I experience and express my feelings. If I don't, the hope fades, the dysfunctional family patterns continue in my own life and forgiveness — true forgiveness — never comes. I finally stopped blaming myself and realized that most of the patterns I demonstrated were learned as a child. I knew I needed to identify those patterns, work on them and take the pressure and guilt off myself for having them. I needed to start forgiving myself. Forgiveness must originate with ourselves before we can extend it to others.

When I ask clients and workshop participants, "Who are you most angry at?" they'll readily say themselves. "I'm angry at myself."

Now there are two major problems with this, other than it being a waste of time to be angry at oneself. First of all, no matter how hard I try, I can't find any pattern of behavior I have that I didn't see my parents, grandparents, uncles, aunts or someone else demonstrate when I was a child. The way I am in relationships (or I should say used to be, thanks to my recovery program) is the way either my mom or dad showed me to be. My way of dealing with money was shown to me by my parents. My understanding or lack of it about sex, as a teenager and young adult, was mostly given to me by my parents, peers or the culture at large.

Now don't misunderstand. It is my responsibility as an adult to correct the behavioral patterns I learned as a child. But first I have to identify them as something that I was taught or not taught, directly or indirectly, by my parents. If I can experience and express my feelings about these destructive patterns that were imprinted into my brain, then I can move out from under them. I can get the information, tools and experience I need and then practice new behaviors, not expecting immediate mastery. If I'm still blaming myself for learning dysfunctional behaviors, then I'm still in denial. I'm turning the energy back on myself, and that's not where it belongs.

Anger, sadness, rage and grief all need to go out of me and be released. But if I'm angry at myself, that energy needing to be released shoots back into my body and mind and serves no useful purpose. I end up storing that anger inside me, instead of freeing up my energy to learn new positive behaviors. By realizing that no one comes into this world demonstrating destructive, self-defeating patterns, but that we learn them from someone, usually someone in our family, we can release the guilt, the blame and the shame. If we keep blaming ourselves for things we learned as children, we don't get anywhere very fast. Once we stop the blaming, we can get to forgiveness of ourselves and of our parents as they were 20, 30 or 40 years ago. Perhaps we can even have a new relationship with them in the present.

Several days after I returned home, all of this hit me as I was walking down the hall in my house. I fell down on my knees, said out loud, "Dad, I love you unconditionally," and wept purifying and cleansing tears. I was happier than I'd been in years. By letting him go — letting my wish for a fantastic father go — I somehow mysteriously got to experience what I'd always wanted, unconditional love. I loved myself and him enough to let go, and when I did, I didn't feel alone.

I had felt strong and clean for days when Lucy called. She was feeling down and depressed about her career, her health and her life. She said she was coming to Austin and wanted to get together and see if we could be friends. As strong as I felt, I thought I could comply.

A few days later she arrived. By the time she got there, I was tense, nervous and angry. I was mad because I knew that we were doing what we always did. I was sliding rapidly into co-dependency, whether she was or not. My strength slipped out of me as it came time for us to get together. Lucy appeared on my doorstep. She came in, and somehow we ended up throwing soft pillows at each other, crying and holding each other in the middle of a house full of memories.

I was so sad that she couldn't be the one. I'm guessing here, but I think she was sad that I couldn't be strong enough to establish and maintain the boundaries I needed to have.

We went to dinner and talked, guardedly at first, and then as it was customary, since she was about to leave, she opened up a bit more. She told me a truth that turned into pain as soon as it left her mouth and reached my heart. "John, I know this may hurt you, but I have to tell you the truth. I love Robert the way you love me. And Robert is not available to me, the way I'm not available to you. Like you are there for me always, I'm there for him. I know that I'll never have him and that it will never work out, but I'm going to try because I love him. And yet in my mind I know that I should be with you."

My body turned into fire. The anger rose in me. As she finished speaking, in my mind's eye I saw myself leaping at her, grabbing her by the throat and choking the life out of her. My eyes pierced her. Her eyes showed her fear of a man who became the father she saw lunge at her mother.

One night, when I was nine, Dad in a fit of rage went for Mom's throat at the dinner table. That sent me into shock for years and made me too scared to ever get angry. After all these years of working, specializing in teaching people how to express anger appropriately, I realized at that moment I was my dad in many ways. I calmed down and didn't carry out the picture in my head that was placed there by a parent long ago. As soon as I did, I realized that now I had to forgive the dad in me. I had to take responsibility never to let such cruelty be perpetuated in the present.

I told Lucy how I felt — angry, very angry. She said she could see and feel my anger. She apologized. I accepted it and her truth and my truth. This woman and I could not be together.

I drove her home and parked in the driveway. The night was clear and warm. Lucy looked at me and touched my hand gently. "John, I want us to be friends . . . good friends. You know that I love you . . . don't you?"

"Lucy, I know that you want to love me. That you want to love somebody. I also know that you've never been loved the way I love you." I paused and took a deep breath.

"John, I do love you. You're special to me." She looked away.

"Lucy, this may sound weird, but it's what I believe and feel. I love you with my body, my heart and my head. I feel that you love me with your head, but not your body and certainly not your heart. I believe that you can feel my love for you. You're probably only the second woman in my life, the other being Penny, my high-school sweetheart, who has fully received it. You know it, you feel it, you count on it and you depend on it. I can't count on your love and I can't let myself need it because it exists only in your mind and not in your body. You don't really love me. You can't. But you know I love you." Tears ran down my face as she turned away once again. "While much of what we do is addictive and co-dependent as hell, I love you and we both know it." Then I looked away and began to get very sad.

"You're right, I can feel your love with my body and mind. I wish I could love you the way you love me, the way Bob (her first love) loved me years go. I just can't. I don't know why. I just can't let it in. I know that I should. I know that you want in. I know you'd make a good husband, father and friend. But in my own way, I do love you."

"You just can't be there for me. And you probably never will. I keep giving us chances and have refused to give up hope that someday you'd stop hurting me and yourself. But you can't love me, and you can't be there."

As I spoke, I had the strangest sensation going through my body and a distinct feeling of déjà vu. Where had this all happened before? Had we done this in another lifetime? Had I said those words before to this woman in a different incarnation on the island of Atlantis?

Then it hit me with tidal-wave force. These were the words, almost verbatim, that Laural had said to me years before. Then I didn't know what she was talking about. Now I understood. She said to me what I was saying to Lucy. I felt some of her pain and frustration that I couldn't ever feel before. I could no more love her at the time, the way she needed to be loved, than Lucy could love me at that moment. I finally felt what she needed me to feel long ago, parked in another car on another night, long after we broke up. I loved Laural with my head. She loved me with heart, body and mind. It was not until after she left me that I went into my body and found the pain and wounds that needed healing before I could love anyone the way they should be loved. I just didn't understand at the time. There was so much pain in those moments, as I began saying goodbye to Lucy and realizing the hurt and pain Laural must have felt.

The Ending

September came and another Texas summer tried to depart about as hard as I tried to leave Lucy.

It's so hard for a co-dependent to tell the one he's addicted to not to call, come by or make contact until they're ready. It's just as hard for many adult children to hear the word "No" as it is for some of us to say it.

"No," it has been said, is the one word the addict hates most to hear. I told Lucy not to call or get in touch when we parted for the third or tenth time — I lost count. She said she wouldn't contact me.

September turned into October. My birthday was at hand, and in my heart and head was the need to hear from Lucy. I thought if she really cared, she'd at least send me a birthday card, in spite of the fact I told her no contact. The birthday card arrived a few days after my birthday — par for the course, she was always late. When it did, I was elated and angry. I was glad she trespassed and acknowledged my birthday, and angry that she trespassed and acknowledged my birthday. A few days later, I came home to find a belated birthday message on my message machine.

So I began thinking maybe I should at least call her and thank her for trespassing. This was as good an excuse as I needed to make contact, have another hit and be co-dependent one more time — as if maybe it would be the last. Being from the South, I'm a real slow learner.

I called and the conversation was the same. "I miss you." "Me too." "I'm sad." "Me too." It doesn't matter who said what. We each said these things in one conversation or another. If I was down when I called, I'd feel better in some ways, and she'd feel down. If she called feeling terrible and I was feeling okay, she'd feel great and I'd be depressed.

As I said before, co-dependency is about energy. It means not having enough to run our own lives on our own steam. We get a person or a thing or a drug to temporarily energize us, just like our addicted parents did. Lucy and I used each other; we didn't support each other. We fed off each other, fueled each other and tried to fool each other as long as we could for as long as we needed to. The disease was about to run its course. Only a couple more encounters, a couple of curtain calls, an encore or two and the music would come to an end.

There's something about that season from Thanksgiving to New Year's that will bring out the adult children's worst fears and greatest expectations. One of the biggest fears is that we'll be alone. The biggest expectation is that we'll finally have a Christmas the way a normal family does. This Christmas we'll all be together, and we'll all love each other and communicate our feelings openly and honestly.

For years I started dreading the approaching Christmas season as early as June. With some work, I finally made it up to September or October before I went into preholiday depression. That's finally changed, but it's often still hard. There's still a little boy in me who wants to believe in Santa Claus and an overnight cure for alcoholism, dysfunction and co-dependency.

Many co-dependent adult children seem to feel absolutely compelled to go home during the holidays, no matter how much they don't really want to.

"Mary, are you going home for Christmas this year?" the therapist asks the Marys and Johns of the world.

"I don't want to. It's always terrible at our house. It's crazy. Mom works herself to death getting the meal prepared. Dad and my brothers stare at endless football games. There's always so much tension in the air you could cut it with a knife. No one really talks to each other and everyone acts like there's nothing wrong. I think I'm the only crazy one in the family because I either want to scream or run away and everyone else looks like everything is fine . . . Yes, I'm going home."

"How is it that you feel you must go if it's so bad?" Therapists who specialize in co-dependency already know, but we ask anyway.

"Mom would be crushed if I didn't. Dad would be so upset. My sisters and brothers would disown me. And my parents always say, 'Grandma isn't going to be with us much longer and is dying to see you. If you can't think of us at least think of her. Don't be so selfish!' "

So adult children go, and everything is pretty much like it's always been. They are so tense they say or hear something that sets things off, and the whole holiday ends up a big mess. Hope that "this time would be different" gets postponed until the next Christmas. No one has a good time except the ones still in denial.

When ACoAs survive the holidays and return to their groups and private sessions, they have lots to work on. So going home does give us therapists plenty to wrestle with from January to the middle of November. Many ACoAs

want three to six extra sessions per week after that if
they can afford them. Most of us really just want someone
to tell us we don't have to go home this Christmas if we
don't want to. Going home can be for some the loneliest
way to spend the holidays. We go to not be alone, and yet
loneliness was exactly what I would feel the most as I
looked at the way our family really was.

As a footnote to all of this, when I didn't go home, I had
a tendency to isolate and white-knuckle my way through
the holidays. Since I didn't feel I fit in anywhere, I'd often
be by myself. People would ask me over for dinner or to
come home with them and be a part of their family. I'd
decline and go to a couple of movies on Thanksgiving,
Christmas and New Year's Day. I always knew the best
pictures to tell folks to see when they returned from
visiting their families.

The bottom line is that no matter what I did to not feel
alone — whether it was to muster up the wherewithal to
go home or stay by myself — I still felt alone.

Last year I didn't do either. I went to Al-Anon and
CoDA meetings during the holidays and felt for the first
time that I was not alone. I fit in. All the meetings were
made up of those of us who were ready to stop going
home and pretending or enduring the ordeal. Yet we were
not hiding out in movie theaters and under the covers in
our bedrooms. It felt great. This year, after three years in
recovery, the holidays were finally happy. But the year
before? . . . Well!!

Christmas 1987: Lucy decided she wanted to try to get
together again, so she called and invited me to her family's
home in Austin for Christmas. I still wanted to be with
that woman more than was reasonable. I liked her family,
and I was ready to try to be with someone other than
myself on Christmas Day.

Her car broke down on the outskirts of town so naturally I volunteered to fix it before dinner. While I worked on it, we talked. She told me she still loved the same unavailable man, which meant I was still loving the same unavailable woman, and I'll tell you I still didn't want to be alone on Christmas.

She and I spent that day together, but I got more from being with her family than I did from her. The kid in me was comfortable with her mom and dad and brothers and sisters. We ate and ate, and we all talked a little in between her mom filling my plate and me filling my mouth. But the man in me wasn't getting what he needed again. This time, though, there was a shift. I could finally distinguish between the two. There was the little boy who wanted the woman to mother him, take care of him and love him and who wanted a family, any family. There was also the man who had genuine healthy needs that included being with a woman who was present, available and desired to be with him as much as he did with her.

This woman had more potential than anyone I'd been with since Laural. (I remembered the dozens of lectures I'd given about loving people with potential.) I couldn't quite let her go and develop all that beautiful potential somewhere else. However, I knew the end of another sad love song was near.

I decided to get more therapy specifically for co-dependency. I began seeing an excellent therapist, and we worked on setting boundaries and healing my addiction-based relationships. Weeks turned into a couple of months, and I began feeling stronger than ever. I decided the only way I'd see Lucy again was if she went into therapy and fully committed herself to a recovery program for ACAs and co-dependents. Well, no sooner had I established that boundary, than I heard from her. She asked to borrow my books and tapes on co-dependency. She was ready to

listen and learn about the disease she now recognized as
hers as well as mine. My heart leaped. I thanked God and
asked her when she'd be coming to Austin next. "Soon,
and I'd like to see you and talk."

"Lucy, I'll see you on the condition that you and I go see
a therapist while you're here," I said in my most nonco-
dependent voice.

One of the ways you can tell when you're in co-dependency or being co-dependent is by listening to your own
voice. When we're frightened or anxious as we're talking
to or being with someone, our voice usually reflects this
by going up a half to a whole octave. We sound about five
years old. This is the voice of the unsafe child who is
afraid something bad is about to happen.

The tension and fear make the vocal chords constrict,
which is accompanied by shallow breathing. The breath
is, of course, a major key to coming out of dependency. By
focusing on the breath, rather than on what the other
person is thinking, feeling or going to say next, you can
often pull yourself out of the co-dependent moment. Try
taking full deep breaths when something or someone is
making you scared. Through the breath, one goes inside
to find the only real source of healing. When we breathe
fully, our bodies relax and we can think and speak clearly.

I've also noticed that when adult children do the emotional release work necessary to recovery, their whole
bodies change. As they release the pent-up anger, rage
and grief they've stored in their bodies for years, they
experience dramatic physical and emotional shifts. I've
witnessed clients' backs become straighter and more
erect. Often their voices drop an octave or two, becoming thicker, deeper, richer and more self-assured. Pre-
mature age and wrinkle lines leave their faces, sex
improves, and energy almost always increases. By find-

ing, knowing, monitoring and loving our bodies, we can greatly enhance our recovery.

She agreed to see a therapist, and we went. Without saying specifically what I heard or saw or felt in that session, I can tell you that I felt so close to her that my boundaries disappeared again. I wanted to believe we could be together and the King's men could put our Humpty Dumpty love affair back together again.

After the session we took a long walk and ended up in a beautiful rose garden. We lay on the cool spring lawn and held each other, alternating between looking into each other's eyes and then into the sky. We talked about the session and what each of us had learned. What I learned was that I shifted between being Lucy's dad or my dad on some days and her mom or my mom on others. Most of the time I was her mom.

I was like her mom and my mom when I'd constantly try one more time to be with her. I was like them when I'd lecture her about her co-dependency and ACoA issues and how they were affecting our relationship. I was like my mom when I made it sound as if she were sick and I were sane. I was like my dad when I wouldn't call or wouldn't give in to her demands.

I was sad and hurt because I just wanted to be me. She just wanted to be herself, though I kept seeing her as my unavailable father. And neither of us wanted to be alone.

One thing I know is that I always wanted to be seen for who I am, not for what I do or look like, sound like or try to act like. My parents never really saw me. They saw what they wanted and needed me to be. I remember Laural wanting so much for me to see her. Instead, I projected onto her my own lost feminine soul or self. I would alternate between making her into my dad one day and my mom the next.

When I was with Lucy, I wanted her to do what my parents could not do — to see me as I really was. She was no more equipped by her parents to do this than I was.

I know that to this day when somebody tries to make me into someone other than myself — a parent, an old boy friend, an old employer — it angers me. It reminds me of childhood. I still long to be taken as I am and not who they need or want me to be.

Adult children need to be loved for who we are, not for what we do. This is a need that some say is impossible to fulfill because it sounds like unconditional love. Most of us didn't receive unconditional love from our parents. We were loved if we were "good," "pretty," "smart," "athletic," "nice," etc. — the list goes on. And if we weren't, we were punished, rejected, shamed, ignored, beaten — abused. So we have little understanding and little training for unconditional love. But I believe we can learn; we can teach ourselves and each other. We can learn to love others unconditionally as we go about learning to love ourselves unconditionally: fat bodies, too tall, non-athletic, not nice, no genius and all. Then perhaps someone else can love us unconditionally, especially if we grieve the fact that the people we loved the most couldn't extend what we needed the most.

Lucy and I talked for about an hour. Then I took her to her car.

"Lucy, if we're to see each other, it has to be on the condition that we continue seeing a therapist together. I'm going to do more individual work on my co-dependency and ACoA issues. In order for us to have any possibility of a relationship, I need you to do the same."

She agreed. I couldn't believe it. Did she really want me enough to comply? Was she really going to be there this time? Could I really count on her this time? Was little Lucy really going to hold the football for good old Charlie Brown to kick without pulling it away at just the right critical moment for me to fall on my ass for the hundredth time, feeling abandoned, embarrassed and bruised? Naw, not Lucy.

The next scheduled sessions she cancelled. We never saw a therapist together again. I lost her again. But I finally found the courage to tell her I didn't want to see her or hear from her again for a long time. Sounds familiar, doesn't it? Well, we went a couple of months. I missed her and I got strong. I needed her and I got weak. I longed for her, but didn't call. Then she did. We talked, we cried, we hurt. But I told her I couldn't see her again.

After a few months, lo and behold, it was the holidays again and she was coming home for Thanksgiving 1988, the recovery time I'd put in was going to be tested. I hoped it would get me through the holidays without as much pain as previous ones. And then I got a phone call.

"I'm coming home for Thanksgiving, and I'd like to see you. My mom told me to tell you to come spend Turkey day with us." Her voice was tentative.

"Is that your way of inviting me to dinner? If you want me to come, ask me. Or is this just your mother's needs?" I said fairly powerfully.

"I'd like it if you'd have dinner with me and my family on Thanksgiving."

"I'll think about it and let you know." I couldn't believe I said that. I almost never "think" about invitations like that.

We decided that she'd call me when she got to town and I'd give her my answer.

We got together, had a great dinner, saw a movie afterward and talked late into the evening about — guess what — our relationship. It was a good talk. We decided there was so much potential, so much good and so much desire to know if we really could be together. She seemed different; more open, more honest, more in touch with her feelings. Mostly she was just much softer and gentler than before.

There still had been no therapy or treatment for co-dependency on her part. I'd done quite a bit, and when she left that evening I was still feeling fine. I didn't feel as if a piece of me had been taken. I felt intact and in hope instead of insecure. I didn't know how she felt, but I knew I was okay. My program and my recovery, while not perfect, were performing miracles right before my eyes. Then came Christmas.

My power was firmly placed in my solar plexus and in my heart. As children that was where our power resided naturally. At an early age our power was drained by parents who needed us to be something or somebody that would make them feel better about themselves. When this occurs, we try to figure out how to survive. We often seek partners for sexual contact only as a means to feel connected in the ways we longed to be with our parents who couldn't be there for us.

When we are asked by our lovers over and over to come from our hearts and our guts, we get frightened. From that place we can feel the fear of being abandoned again. I longed to love and be loved, and women longed for me to come from my heart when I came to them. I couldn't. I lost Laural and others because I couldn't. But most impor-tantly I lost my "self."

My recovery process, my healing journey, was allowing me to reside for longer periods in that sacred temple called the heart, after all those years of inability to be anything but a momentary visitor. By going into the pain, feeling the abandonment in childhood and wrestling with fear of being left alone again, I was now beginning to truly live in my body. The power was returning. I was reclaiming the power I had given up to be in relationships with people who could not be with me. The energy that was my birthright was returning, moment by moment, hourly, daily. I was returning to my heart's home. I was returning to myself. This time there would really be someone at home waiting for me . . . myself.

My co-dependency, which had plagued every relationship I'd ever had, was diminishing in its intensity and lessening its grip on my life. The times I was co-dependent were decreasing. And when I was co-dependent, I could recover my sanity much more quickly than I used to.

Two years ago, when I'd go on a co-dependent binge with women, food, work, alcohol or whatever, it would take me a long time to see it and then sober up. I use the same term as that of an alcoholic because co-dependency is a lot like drinking or drugging. You quit, you get on the wagon and, just like an alcoholic, you fall off from time to time. When I do, I feel heavy for a while, complete with tiredness, lethargy and low self-esteem. Then I go to meetings, get support, work my program, be around safe people, and I sober up from the disease of co-dependency. Each time I do, I learn something about myself.

When I'd get in touch with Lucy or she would get in touch with me, it felt like playing with fire or firewater. How much could I drink in before I'd fall into that flame, burn my boundaries, give up my power and become needy and co-dependent as hell? And then how long would it take to recuperate, regenerate and realize what I'd done? Due to recovery, it happened less and less frequently. I was changing, I was healing and I was letting go.

Lucy called two weeks before Christmas. I was planning to go south for the holidays, visit some friends and see my mom, though I had decided not to do the family thing this time. However, I had to go through Mississippi on my way and had mentioned this to Lucy at Thanksgiving.

"Hi! How you doing?" She asked in her most upbeat voice.

"Fine. And you?"

"Great!"

Now I could tell you the details but you've already guessed the results. I was going to Mississippi one more time with a hope that this time would be different. It was. But at first it was the same old story.

I got there, and she wasn't feeling well. This reminded me of my mom, who was sick a lot when I was a kid. I got through this without too much projection. But all the plans we had made, on the telephone line that always brought us so close, were cancelled when I got there in person.

After staying two nights in a hotel, alone, frustrated and slightly angry, I decided to leave the next morning while I still had enough strength, power and anger to get me to Alabama. She called that morning.

"Look, I'm going to get on the road," I said. "This ain't working out. I'm glad I got to see you a little while. You take care and I'll see you later." I spoke the words with a sharp edge to each one.

"I'm sorry it didn't work out," she replied.

"Me too. I'll see you later."

"Will you come back by on your way back to Texas?" Her voice sounded so sad.

"I'll see. I've got to go. Goodbye."

I hung up the phone and thought, "Hmm! I don't feel too bad this time. I'm all right. I'm not dead. I feel pretty strong. I think I've really got rid of the co-dependency thing. I think I'll call her back before I leave and tell her I'm definitely not coming back and I won't be seeing her again."

Just at that moment I heard "Mr. Lee, Mr. John Lee. Phone call in the lobby."

I picked up the phone. "John, I really want to give you something before you leave. I have this special Christmas present I've been wanting you to have for a long time. Will you come over long enough to get it and say goodbye?"

Tell me, what did I say? You know by now, don't you?

"Yes." "Yes." "Yes." "Yes." What else can a co-dependent say?

We agreed to meet at a cafe near her house and my hotel. When I arrived, she, who was always late, was standing on the corner to meet me in her prettiest dress and looking like a million dollars. My heart turned to mush. My boundaries turned into dust. My power flew right out of my body and I hugged hers.

She handed me my present. It was an Oriental box, the kind that I collect. I was deeply touched.

I looked at her and touched her lightly on the hand. "Would you tell me what you want me to know before I leave? If there's something you need to say, I'll listen." I asked in a very serious tone.

"I don't want to talk," she snapped.

"Fine. Just fine. Then don't."

A few strained moments went by. "I've been thinking about moving back to Austin," she said.

My mouth fell open. "What for? Your work is here. Your friends are here. You don't want to live in Austin. Why would you consider moving there?" My question was sincere.

"To see if we could work things out and be together." She said, looking out of the window.

"You're kidding. You've really thought about that. I didn't know. I had no idea." My enthusiasm was obvious.

"I've thought a lot about it. I don't think I can leave here just yet, but I have wondered. I want to see you again. Will you come back this way on your way home? We could get together. I'm sure I'll be feeling better by then, and we can spend some time and get to know each other better. I've changed a lot and I sense you have, too. You seem to be much gentler and happier with yourself than when I first met you. And I'm getting softer all the time."

I looked at her and said . . . "Yes."

When I left her, I was full of hope and full of trust. I thought this time we could make it.

Well, to make much too long a story short, I called from Birmingham. We were as far away as if I were calling from Africa. She couldn't arrange her schedule to see me except for a few hours on a Saturday. And then once again, I was disappointed, co-dependent as hell, and my neediness leaked out over the telephone line. She said, "I've been thinking all I can do is just be friends, and I can see you want more. I only have a couple of hours that I can spend, and it's obvious you're in that needy co-dependent place. I'm okay. I'm sorry you're not. I do want to be your friend."

I hung up the phone and felt the pain for about an hour. I breathed deep breaths, got real still and real quiet and asked my inner child what he really needed. He replied "I don't need this any more." I really heard him. Over the months, I had again learned to listen to this gentle voice and ask him about many things. I practiced listening and responding when he'd tell me he was tired, hungry, needing to play or be around safe supportive people. I was learning how to be present for myself. His voice was loud and clear: "I don't need this any more."

I knew the only way I'd ever feel alone again was if I stopped listening to this voice. I knew that if I stopped numbing the Holy voice with work, sex, alcohol and addictive processes, I wouldn't be alone. The child within was still alive and kicking. The child and the man who I am began to take hands. The child began to feel secure that nothing or no one was going to hurt him, abandon him or abuse him again. The man knew that the part of him he had always missed was returning. It would allow him to be open to loving, safe, supportive people. By listening to and nurturing my own inner child, I knew that I would never be alone. I let nothing or no one come between me and my recovery. I could finally be with the child, with God, with nature and other people willing to love me as I am. I knew that recovery is a process and that life still would not be perfect, but I knew it would never again be as painful.

New Beginnings

Since that little boy's voice was heard, I haven't needed to call Lucy or be called by her. I've been fine. I've been dancing in my dining room alone for a few months now. It's over. It's really finished. I love her. But it's over and I feel great. And for the first time since before I met her, I'm having a relationship with myself.

I have noticed that most adult children start at what I call the wrong end of love. We need love and need to give love so much that we start at the most difficult, scary, risky place. We start with one other person who becomes our everything, even our Higher Power, mostly because we feel so empty. Before we have learned how to be intimate and close to a friend or a group, to nature or to a God, we go right for that special person. Most of us have failed pretty miserably at the task of loving ourselves, so we try to find someone else to love us the way we can't. Even before we grieve the fact that our parents couldn't love us the way we needed, we go looking for a stranger to do what they could not.

In recovery I have learned that I have to work up to being able to love another person. This is the highest and deepest love, other than love for God and oneself. So I started by working on my ability to share and be open, honest and intimate with friends, ACoA and CoDA groups, colleagues, and others before going to the heart of one other person. As I became more able to truly reveal myself to others, where the risks of rejection were not so outrageous, I realized that I could trust myself with others and be trusted. It's very scary to try to be intimate with anyone, but to try and go from an inability to love onself to loving another is a large leap. It often has us landing in divorce court. Perhaps we need to start at the end where there's not as much at stake, where we can develop our skills at communication, sharing, giving and receiving attention and nurturing. This way we start loving ourselves first. Then it might be easier to love someone else. An added extra benefit is then if the relationship doesn't work out, we'll still have a relationship with ourselves.

I have realized that until we are able to let our parents go, we can't let go of the other people we love. I still have much to work on and feel, but now I know I have truly forgiven and unconditionally love my dad and mom. I can't be with Dad yet and feel safe, as he is in the process of spiraling downward into the latter stages of alcoholism. So my dad and I have no relationship at this point. Mom, who is deep in recovery and goes to Al-Anon meetings and therapy regularly, is doing better than ever.

She and I have a beautiful, different, healthy relationship. But I had to let her go to get this, and she had to let me go. I include two excerpts from her last two letters as examples of her and my metamorphosis:

First letter:

> My beloved Son, you will never realize how much I love you. And if you ever need me, I'll be there for you. I'll

always be grateful to you for starting me on my road to recovery. And you did it as a healthy man helping a woman who happens to be your mother find some peace and serenity in her old age.

Second letter:

John, I'm so thankful for my program. Learning the difference in caretaking, taking care of . . . Learning how to take care of myself has really been an experience. I have so much to learn and am very eager to learn. God has been so good to me. I still have some bad times, but the lows aren't so low anymore. It's wonderful not to be depressed all the time . . . The only thing that helps me is gratitude. It seems like the longer I'm in recovery, the more grateful I am for everything, even for being alone. It's like God has given me a time for peace, to learn and to live without thinking that it takes another person to make me happy . . . For me, it's like waking up a little at a time.

The sick part of me still wishes I could fix Kathy, Randy, Jim or anyone else I think needs fixing, but the well part breathes a sigh of relief just knowing that the only one I have to and can fix is me . . . I think I must be a couple of inches taller just taking that load off my back.

I love you,
Mom

To get to this place with my mom and dad, I had to do something I didn't do with Lucy until that last December. I had to detach.

For adult children the word "detach" itself causes terror and confusion. Until we learn what it means, we try to do it while we're still enmeshed with the person we're trying to detach from. I tried to be friends with Lucy without truly detaching. It didn't work. I had to take the time necessary to heal and discharge all the old emotions around the thing we called a "love relationship."

Adult children try hard to be friends with their former lovers or partners. It sounds something like this: "Okay. I know we can't be lovers any more, but I want to be good friends." For many ACoAs their partners are their only friends. ACoAs don't let that many people in close. When

ACoAs do get involved, they tend to move away from all the other relationships they have formed as soon as they are in a "relationship." When you don't see ACoAs or Co-dependents at meetings for a while, it's usually because they've begun a new relationship. Unfortunately they often show up six months later, ready to begin work again, but wondering why their program of recovery didn't see them through.

So adult children try to be friends before they detach and put some distance between themselves and the past. It doesn't usually work, but it almost always hurts. Time and distance are necessary in the processes of healing and letting go. I remember after Laural and I broke up, I'd wait a month and then call her, promising I was ready to be "just friends." I'd talk her into seeing me. It always hurt us both, but I just didn't want to let go.

A few years ago, I had to tell my mother, "Mom, I don't want to see you for a while." This hurt her and scared me, but it was absolutely necessary. From that moment of detachment, that cutting of the cord, we were allowed space to heal, to forgive and to begin creating something new. It worked. But I had to find the courage to let go and learn that neither she nor I would die. Indeed we live fuller lives than ever, rather than merely surviving, and we love each other more than ever.

I wanted to be with Lucy and detach all in the same moment. It just doesn't work that way. Now that we've let go, we've allowed the healing creative Spirit to move. We both have finally given up our childhood urge to control the present and the future. We've let go.

And now I understand why Dad has taken every drink that has passed over lips unable to form the word "No." I understand why Mom kept putting up with all the bullshit for so long. I understand why Laural saw me every time she did, until she didn't. I understand why I had to have every encounter with Lucy that I had before I stopped. That's the way co-dependents, alcoholics, women who love too much, men who are addicted to women have to be — until they don't have to. Until the moment comes which demands detaching and letting go of the fear of being alone, we continue. No one can stop us but ourselves. That moment comes for each of us in its own time and place. Now I understand, now I forgive and now I can let go.

Now I don't feel alone. I have a beautiful inner child who is more precious than gold and more substantial and special than silver. I have supportive, nurturing, healthy people, both men and women, who love me. They have always loved me for who I am, not for what I do or become. There are ACoA, Al-Anon and CoDA meetings all over this country filled with people who know me. They know that the struggles I go through as an adult child still prove my being co-dependent. They listen and they care, as I have learned to listen to and care deeply for them.

I finally have a relationship with myself for the first time since the cradle. I love myself and I take pretty damn good care of myself. (I still tend to work too much but I'm loving myself through that.) And I have made a pact with myself: I won't compromise my integrity, my inner child or my recovery to be with someone as I had to do as a child.

With all this support and love around me, and with my increasing ability to let it and people in, I no longer have to fear being alone. Adults cannot be abandoned; only I can abandon myself and my inner child. I'm learning every day the ways I do that. As I learn, I continue to decrease the self-abusive behavior I learned as a child living in a dysfunctional family. It is these behavior patterns and thinking that keep me separate from myself, others and my God. As I go deeply into recovery, the patterns lessen their hold on me. The pain is acknowledged, experienced, expressed and released.

You know, the truth is I'm happy most of the time. Less and less do I need someone or something to make me feel that way, I just am. Thank you, God!!! Thank you, Al-Anon, ACoA, CoDA, my teachers, my friends, my clients and you, my readers. Thanks for sharing and listening to my experience, strength and hope.

Postscript

February 1989:

It's been a long time since I've seen Lucy. I didn't call and neither did she for almost a year. I learned that she did go fully into recovery and received treatment for co-dependency and her adult child issues. We talked on the phone after that, and I knew we had finally allowed ourselves the time to heal. We were both getting the recovery we needed, and we really could finally be friends.

We talk every few months or so now. When we do, we heal some old wounds. We share the present feelings, insights, joys and successes which are part of our individual recovery journeys. We're starting to trust each other, while we remain true to ourselves and committed to our recovery. We're becoming good friends. We've let go. I'm doing fine and she seems to be doing really well. I'm still sad from time to time that we couldn't make it as partners and lovers, but I'm thankful to God for what I learned, what I felt, and for my recovery.

Many of you who read my first book have been kind enough to write letters or ask at workshops, "Whatever happened to Laural? Did she like the book? Did you ever get back together?"

This is what happened:

Laural stopped talking to me and seeing me right after the book came out. To my knowledge, she has no idea of the many thousands of copies it's sold and the many people who have said it has helped them on their own healing journey.

She did not like the book for several reasons. One is because I did not tell the story the same way she would have. She also felt her privacy had been invaded. I wish I could have written a book she could have loved, as much as I wish I could have got her to come back. She never did come back. I never really let go of the hope that some day she might until recently.

I want to share with you briefly the last two years of saying goodbye to a woman I loved more than she'll ever know.

The process began with dreams two years ago. In the first dream, I went to the home she then shared with another man. I told them both how much I loved her and told her how much I wanted to be with her.

For two years I dreamed of Laural nearly every week and without exception thought of her a little every day. Even the night that I asked Lucy to marry me, I remember a little voice inside my head saying, "You still love Laural and you'll have to let her go some day."

The dreams kept coming. The feelings of sadness, grief and anger would come up in waves that sometimes I thought I would drown in. Sometimes missing her would get so bad I'd try not to feel the pain, which only made it worse. For a while I tried to exorcise her like a demon from my body and mind until I realized how cruel that was to both of us. Her love ran through my body like blood because we had entered each other's bodies, hearts and souls long ago. Such love is not to be forgotten or got rid of. It is to be cherished and used to love again.

I continued to have a love affair with Laural in my head and my heart. I realize now that, in part, this kept me from being open to a relationship with a real flesh-and-blood person who could be compatible. Laural became my ghostly lover who visted me in my dreams for years. I didn't see her or talk to her except at night, which became the time we could still be together. I'd dream of her, then wake up and cry with longing and sadness that it was only a dream. I kept going to therapy, dealing with my pain and feeling love for this woman. But in the present, she had no idea what I'd become or how much she had played a part in my healing and my helping others to heal similar wounds.

In October, 1987, the month of my birth, on the day of my birth I sent her a letter. The letter simply said I wanted to know if she had any feeling or need to be with me in any way. I asked her to please let me know if there was and I said I was ready for anything: to be friends, partners, lovers or married. When I put the letter in the box, I knew intuitively that I had to put a time limit on it. I could not wait any longer. I needed very much to move on and open up to the present more fully than I had with regard to love and relationships. Something deep inside said to give it until January. I let the letter go, and the grief and the dreams came. I cried many tears as I made the passage from the past to the present.

January came and I received no communication. Hope was fading. Then came a series of dreams:

Dream 1

I was gathered in a circle in a teepee with five other Caucasian men and six American Indian men. We had come for one purpose only — to tell each other how we really felt. Each man in his own turn told of his greatest sorrow. When it came my turn, sitting shirtless, I leaned over backwards with arms outstretched, screamed a scream of grief that shattered the silence of the psyche and spoke the words, "I love Laural." When I awoke, I wept with happiness at the obvious positive symbolism of the dream and with sadness about the one I loved.

Dream 2

A couple of nights later Laural and I were together as we had been in so many dreams before. We were happy and holding each other. I asked her to come back and told her how much I had changed. She said that I hadn't and left. I got down on my knees and clasped my hands together in prayer and cried out to God to please let her come back. I awoke and cried for some time. But I also awoke to a truth that had been kept from me, like a secret everyone else knew. I realized that I really truly loved Laural.

For years I was afraid that I just wanted her because I couldn't have her and that if I ever got her back, it wouldn't be any different. I was always afraid, and I realize now that I did everything I could to make sure she didn't come back. I don't know whether she wanted to come back or not. But I do know that a man who really wants to be with the woman he loves does whatever it takes to enhance the possibility. I refused to leave her alone and continued to hold onto her, psychically if not physically. I think she always felt my firm grasp. I knew that for her to come back I had to let her go. Since I wouldn't let go, I didn't really want her to come back until I knew that I'd be okay without her. I knew I was learning to love that part of me that Laural represented in my dreams. In letting that part go, I could let the person Laural go without losing my love for her as a person.

Dream 3

We got together and once again were very happy. I asked her if she would date me. To my surprise she said yes, and then she left. I awoke and cried.

Dream 4

We were together and looking for a house to move into. We found one on a beautiful sandy beach that looked out over the ocean. She always loved water. We looked inside the house, and I asked her to live with me. She said yes and then left. I awoke and again was happy with the healing symbolism of the dream and sad that it was daylight and no Laural was beside me. The end of January was nearing, and there had been no contact.

Dream 5

Laural and I agreed to see a therapist, but he did not show up for the appointment. She left and I went back, but the therapist could not help. I left and went to see a woman therapist who was very unusual and weird. I left her office and went into a waiting room where several of her colleagues were gathered. She said I was deeply traumatized. I looked her in the eyes and then looked at the others present and said, "I'm not traumatized. I just love a woman and miss her very much."

Dream 6

Laural and I were at a hotel, and I left her in the room again to go to see a therapist. First I saw a male therapist, who could not help me, and then a female therapist. She looked at me and said these words: "You must let Laural go if you really love her. It's the only way. It's what she needs." In the dream I wept and went back to the hotel room. Laural and I held each other and we both cried. I held her tightly and told her, "I love you so much that I have to let you go."

She looked at me and wrapped her whole body around mine as I stood by the door ready to leave. In all the dreams before (I'm sure more than a hundred) she was always the one who left. As I stood there at the door she said, "You really do love yourself now." I cried and said, "Yes, I do, not in the selfish way I did when I was with you but in a healthy way. I love myself enough to let you go."

"I can see that you do, and I too have to learn to love myself in that way." The dream ended. I awoke and cried tears from the bottom of my sad joyful heart. I knew I was really ready to let her go.

There were still a few days of January left. During every one of those last seven or eight days I thought about calling her at the least and going to find her at the most. And then I understood something I'd never known before.

I had a long talk with my good friend and partner, Bill Stott. I told him about the dreams, the tears and the torment. I told him I thought perhaps I should call her. But I knew if I did, she'd be right that I hadn't really changed because that's what I always did. I always called her or another woman to try to fix myself or to be my soul for me. I always went out to her, and she always said she would come to me if it was right and I would have to trust that to be so. I was big on control, small on trusting.

"If you call her, she will just feel you are being cruel." Bill said the words without awareness of their wisdom.

"My God, I never realized that!"

"Perhaps she doesn't want to talk to you because she's still afraid," he said. "If you call, she has no control over her hurt, and once again you'll be controlling her."

As Bill talked I remembered two things. One was that she used to say when I'd call, "You just won't stop hurting me." I never understood what she meant, since it always made me feel better to get in touch.

The second thing I remembered was how hurt I would be when Lucy would call me or we would get together. She could not love me, and she could not let me go. This hurt and angered me so much, and I thought how cruel she was not to just leave me alone so I could heal my wounds.

It all came together in that moment. I was released from a pattern that had held me prisoner for so long. I realized that the last thing I wanted was to hurt her any more. I was ready to love her genuinely enough to let her go and never contact her or be cruel again. It was done. The urge for physical contact was all but gone. It was virtually finished, and I was delivered from the pain I'd been carrying for years. I knew that I really did love her enough to let her go. I knew that kind of love could only come to someone who finally stops using people to feel good. It comes to those who finally love themselves enough to know they won't be alone, so they are no longer terrified of being abandoned.

I finally felt the words of the wise Chinese sage, Confucius, that I'd read years before and regarded as beautiful but enigmatic. *"If he had loved her, he wouldn't have minded the distance."* I never really got their meaning until that moment.

I really loved her. I really had to let her go. And I knew that the distance was diminished as the illusion disappeared that we people are separate. True love is the eternal connecting force stronger than any will to control another. It is this love that is "The Bridge Across Forever."

A couple of weeks after the last of those six dreams, I realized I would never physically intrude on Laural's life again without specific invitation. I knew without a shadow of a doubt that I loved this woman and in that love wanted only her highest good. If that meant no contact, then I'd still live and be happy.

Dream 7

I received a phone call. Her tender voice was on the other end of the line, and she said only the words, "Please help me."

I woke up confused and co-dependent. Was she in trouble? Was this a psychic plea for me to contact her? Did she need rescuing? I wanted to believe that the answer to all these questions was my formerly favorite word, "yes." But after reflection and feeling I knew the answer was no. I knew in my heart that the plea was for me to now let go of the psychic connection we had. I had to love her enough to really let her go, so she would finally feel free and feel loved by me.

It became clear that what I needed to do now was what she had done for herself and for me almost five years ago. She loved us both enough to let me go. Had she not, I know I wouldn't be where I am today, and I wouldn't trade where I am for anything or anybody. Now it was time to let my ghostly lover go and give up the psychic connection as well. It was time to say goodbye. It was time to let the dream go.

It was time to acknowledge that Laural, who had long symbolized unconditional love for me, was now in me.

Her gentleness and tenderness were a part of me. The
Laural in my dreams was my feminine side, longing to be
recognized, nurtured and embraced. I was ready to accept
that side of myself and let the flesh-and-blood Laural go.

I sat down in the middle of my writing room and prayed.
I asked Laural for forgiveness and God for the strength to
do what I needed to. I imagined myself sending beautiful
white light to Laural and wrapping myself in it as well, and
with arms raised to the sky I released her in love. The
anger had long since died. The fear of being alone was
gone, as was the guilt I used to connect us. I got up and
wrote for four hours, knowing that I had to finish this
book and close the door to the past. By finishing the book,
I would leave behind the past with the Laural I used to
know and the Lucy I thought I knew but didn't. It was time
to move fully into the present and experience the joy and
ecstasy waiting for this recovering co-dependent adult child
of an alcoholic. I finally fully realized I didn't need fixing
anymore because I wasn't broken. Therefore I didn't "need"
a woman to make me whole. The woman I needed was the
feminine aspect of myself that I'd denied for so long.

I'm ready to journey into the unknown now. Perhaps I
will travel with a partner if she waits, or perhaps I will be
by myself. But I won't be alone because you'll also be on
this journey. I'll see you there. You'll come in your own
time and in your own way. We will recognize each other
and hold each other's hands when it gets scary. The truth
is *I Don't Want to Be Alone*, and I can open up now so I don't
have to be. You can, too. Take real good care of yourself.
I'll see you.

God Bless You,

John

Cassette Tape Series

. . . is available from John Lee at Austin Men's Center, 700 West Avenue, Austin, Texas, 78701. Phone: (512) 477-9595. In a powerful and humorous way, these tapes help you make sense out of the emotional confusion caused by growing up in an alcoholic or dysfunctional family. Titles include:

- Why Men Can't Feel And The Price Women Pay
- Expressing Your Anger Appropriately
- Grieving, A Key To Healing
- Healing The Father-Son Wound
- What Co-dependency Really Is
- Addictive Relationships
- Saying Goodbye To Mom And Dad
- Couples, Caring And Co-dependency
- The Flying Boy: Healing The Wounded Man Workshop
  (3 tapes at $24.95 plus $2.50 for postage/handling)

Tapes are $9.95 each plus $1.95 for postage/handling.
Texas residents add 8% sales tax.